'Full of new information – as always engagingly written.'
Jane Clifton, *New Zealand Listener*

'A wonderful read – even better than *I've been thinking.*'
Rt Hon Mike Moore

'Richard has real insights into business sucess.'
Don Braid, Managing Director
Mainfreight

'Richard Prebble has been one of New Zealand's remarkable leaders and this book shows how he did it.'
Sir Roger Douglas

OUT OF THE RED

Hon Richard Prebble

© Richard Prebble 2006. All rights are reserved. No part of this book may be reproduced other than for the purpose of academic study or review without the permission of the author.

Published by:
The Letter Limited
45 State Highway 30
Rotoma
Rotorua, 3074
www.theletter.biz

The headline on page 92 is reproduced by permission of the *Wanganui Chronicle*, 17 October 1986.
The headline on page 95 is reproduced by permission of the *New Zealand Herald/APN*, 25 July 1984.
The headlines on page 99 are reproduced by permission of *Fairfax Sunday Newspapers Auckland Star*, 5 February 1988; the *New Zealand Herald/APN*, 6 February 1988 and the *New Zealand Women's Weekly*, 8 February 1988.
The headlines on page 149 are reproduced by permission of the *New Zealand Herald/APN*, 21 December 1988 and 7 January 1989.
The headlines on page 157 are reproduced with permission of the *Press*, 2 June 1999 and the *Otago Daily Times*, 11 August 1999.

Designed and typeset by Egan Reid Ltd, Auckland
Cover Design: Sue Ryan
Printed in China

ISBN: 0-473-11249-3

A catalogue record for this book is available from the National Library of New Zealand.

The publishers have made every reasonable effort to locate the copyright holders of the photograph on page 41 in this book. If you have any information regarding the copyright of this photograph then please contact the publishers.

Back cover photograph courtesy of ACT New Zealand.

To the New Zealanders who by their efforts turned the state's enterprises into successful companies.

Contents

Introduction	9
Dropped right into it	13
The touchy-feely man	19
Desert survival	26
It is how you think	31
Solutions are the problem	35
The achieving society	39
Clay Lafferty	44
So much for the theory	48
Saving rail	58
Implementing change	73
Achieving change	84
Minister of almost everything	95
Problem-solving	103
Putting out fires	106
Group decision-making	113
Out of the red	119
Failure	133
It's culture that counts	144
The uselessness of audit	165

Seeing ourselves	168
Organisational culture	176
The art of negotiation	181
Boards	200
Conclusion	209
Test your organisation	211
Your results	214

Introduction

'THIS IS NOT what I had in mind.'

I found myself in front of Mr Justice Gendall in the High Court in Wellington. Two high-powered lawyers acting for New Zealand Post were asking the judge that I be issued with an injunction to prevent me from questioning New Zealand Post's business plan. The lawyers further asked for the court to order me to hand over any information I had about their plans for the taxpayers' asset.

'As one of the architects of the state-owned enterprise model who converted government trading departments into businesses registered under the Companies Act,' I told the judge. 'I had intended that the businesses would be more accountable.'

Fortunately the judge threw out the injunction so I did not have to write this book from jail. But it did make me decide to research how well parliament does scrutinise state-owned enterprises (SOEs).

The answer is not good. MPs have largely ignored the business plans and have instead questioned the expenses of the chairman of New Zealand Post; these, I have to admit,

Served with a writ by New Zealand Post on the steps of Parliament – 2001. (*Dominion Post*)

were pretty spectacular. But even Ross Armstrong's use of his credit card did not dent the balance sheet. I have reached the gloomy conclusion that politicians will always be more interested in newsreaders' salaries than in the huge drop in TVNZ's capital value – which is more than a billion dollars in the last six years.

Indeed, I could not find an example of MPs, as opposed to ministers, ever being good at monitoring government businesses. The fact that politicians are hopeless at business is not news. Besides, I have already written that book. What

INTRODUCTION

is interesting is *why* New Zealand was able to turn around its basket-case state businesses. I think we discovered some remarkable things about what causes success that is worthy of another book.

I could not have written this book without a lot of help. My editor Simon Carr has improved this book immeasurably. My secretary Sandy Grove, in her own time, patiently went though each draft. Chris Milne my former chief of staff read the draft and made many corrections. My multi-talented former secretary Sue Ryan produced the cover and edited the draft to produce the final version. Michael Bassett and Mike Moore picked up some of my errors. Roger Douglas clarified certain parts of the Lange story that had become obfuscated.

I would also like to thank Egan Reid Ltd for doing a wonderful job in producing the book.

My friend Michael Gourley corrected many of my mistakes and made many suggestions. I am grateful to him for making available to me copyright Human Synergistics material (which may not be reproduced without approval).

As they say, any wisdom in this book I owe to others and the mistakes are all my own.

Dropped right into it

'YOUR JOB FROM Monday is to be in charge of twenty-one different business disasters. The businesses employ tens of thousands of employees, most of whom are angry and underpaid or angry and underemployed. Their combined output is worth 10 per cent of the nation's GDP, and they're chewing through the wealth of the country at the rate of a billion dollars a year. Most have never made a profit or paid a dividend in their entire existence. Their levels of service would be comical by the standards of the Malagasy Republic. Their products might have looked futuristic in 1965. They are so far behind the rest of the world that they have made us an object of international ridicule. And the managers – of whom there are many – say they need an immediate injection of capital equal to the Government of New Zealand's annual budget.'

'You are to turn all the businesses around into profit within three years. Service standards are to be lifted promptly to equal the best in the world. You must start paying the shareholders a dividend as soon as you may find convenient.'

The prime minister, David Lange, when he appointed me

to be the first minister of state-owned enterprises, did not use these words. As I recall, he said something like: 'The government's businesses are an absolute mare's nest. I want you to see if you can fix them up.'

My relations with our enormous prime minister were pretty cordial in those days. But even so, I have a politician's sense of what can and can't be done. You hear the bugle call, your spine tingles, you look up the valley to where the Russian guns are glinting in the distance, and a lot of thoughts go through your mind. Immediately, you consider the merits of a cup of tea. But sometimes the best description of politics is 'the art of the impossible', and so, a little reluctantly and with no little trepidation, you turn your mount up the valley; you ignore the small, nasty little voice in your head questioning whether the prime minister actually wants you to succeed at all . . .

The full, inside story of what happened with those twenty-one businesses has never been told. There have been a number of academic studies and analyses of what came to be known as the SOE model. I've told part of the story myself. But no one knows about the body of ideas that drove the new enterprises. They weren't mine, and weren't even from New Zealand. The managers and directors of the state-owned enterprises weren't exposed to 'Human Synergistics' directly, but indirectly they were, through me. It sounds like a strange cult. That was how Robert Muldoon tried to characterise it. The ideas that sounded eccentric twenty years ago are in the mainstream now, but still they haven't been popularised. They constitute a management practice that can transform the way large companies are organised.

DROPPED RIGHT INTO IT

I'd trained and practised as a lawyer. I'd been an MP for twelve years. I'd been a minister for three years. That spring morning, I walked into the prime minister's office still fairly green. I walked out the biggest businessman in New Zealand's history – as the chief executive of twenty billion dollars' worth of business (about one hundred billion in today's dollars). I was in charge of the country's air, road and rail systems, its national post office and phone company, half the country's forests, all the Landcorp farms, an insurance company, a bank, a computer company, all the nation's electricity generation and the national grid, air traffic control, a property company and a printing works. It's just as well I'm such a modest fellow; twenty billion dollars is the sort of thing that can go to a man's head.

There it was. The nation's silver. A terrible liability. Every one of those businesses losing money hand over fist. Millions of dollars a day – tens of millions on a bad day.

I needed to know what makes an organisation succeed. I needed to know fast. When time is short (and it's always later than you think) you have to act on principle. You've got to get the essence of it right and let the details take care of themselves. My principles of management came, as I say, from the American consultancy whose representative on earth – or at least in New Zealand – was Michael Gourley. We'd already applied the principles in a small way here and there – not least to the cabinet – with some success. The state-owned enterprises were the big test, perhaps the biggest test these principles have ever had.

Three years later, all twenty-one businesses were profitable. Service standards had become world class. Air New

> The transformation of SOEs into leading-edge organisations is one of the biggest business turnarounds ever, anywhere in the world.

Zealand's planes took off on time and the cost of airline tickets had dropped so dramatically that record numbers of passengers were flying. It was a story repeated everywhere. New Zealand Rail, which had been referred to as less efficient than All India Railways, was described by the World Bank as the world's most efficient national narrow-gauge railway.

The transformation of SOEs into leading-edge organisations is one of the biggest business turnarounds ever, anywhere in the world.

The architects of the turnaround make quite a list; a number still make a good income advising on how to reform government businesses. When I am in America people ask me if I know Maurice McTigue. He is the minister who invented the SOE model, they say admiringly. 'Yes, I know him well,' I say. What I do not say is that he was the opposition spokesman who opposed every reform with the ferocity of a fighting cat.

A number of the state businesses have commissioned books to celebrate their success. In their view, their success could not be due to the Treasury or the politicians (a reasonable view) so it must be due to the board, the management and staff. The Reserve Bank governor, Alan Bollard, has co-authored a book that says that any mug can do it. The success could not be due to the businessmen or the politicians; it was apparently all due to Treasury, the deregulation and the SOE model. I think that Geoffrey Palmer should have been given much of the credit for the SOE legislation, a remarkable piece of lawmaking.

If three-sided beings had a god it would be a triangle. In fact, all these explanations have some truth, but none has nailed the essence of it. A recent study shows that the state-owned electricity system is again only half as efficient as the private sector. We're back where we started. The appointment of businessmen to the SOE boards hasn't prevented a steady deterioration: politicians can't resist appointing cronies, or being politically correct. The gender and racial balance on our SOE boards is of international standard; the balance sheets are getting dowdier every year. The boards are political creations and reflect political priorities.

If the SOE model was the transforming idea, all these businesses would still be as successful as they were in 1990, out-performing the stock exchange average. But as they are all drifting lower and lower below that average we have to look elsewhere for the explanation.

In fact, the SOEs are as good or

To turn losing businesses into profitable efficient enterprises you must change the negative thinking of the companies to an achievement culture.

as bad as the culture they create allows them to be. A company creates a culture, then the culture creates the company. To turn losing businesses into profitable efficient enterprises you must change the negative thinking of the companies to an achievement culture. It's easier said than done. But it's something we'll need to do again. Maybe it's something we need to do now.

Over the last decade, New Zealand has enjoyed unprecedented prosperity; we've had a very good run. But for the last five years our growth rate has remained static. How long is that going to last? To lift our prosperity to a new level, to have New Zealand firms succeed internationally, to have world-class education and health services, we need to change our culture, how we react and think about our world.

> **Can you turn a failure around and make it a success?**

We need to discover again why some people succeed. Why do most people fail? Why are a few people leaders? Why are most people followers? Why are some leaders followers? Can you pick who will lead and whose leadership will succeed? Why do a few businesses make wonderful success stories but most fail to make any real progress? Can you turn a failure around and make it a success?

Let's look at the turnaround of the state's enterprises to see if there are lessons we can apply today.

The touchy-feely man

I WAS INTRODUCED to the idea of 'achievement thinking' by the man the former prime minister Muldoon called Labour's 'touchy-feely' man, Michael Gourley.

I was looking for a volunteer to manage my election campaign. This person had to have the ability to produce a campaign plan and then the personality to persuade up to four hundred volunteers to give their time to work constructively to make the campaign a success.

Good campaign managers are not easy to find. There's never enough money, people or time. The people you have are not those that any rational person would have chosen. Good campaign managers turn the most unlikely individuals into an achieving team. A bad campaign manager can pull defeat from the jaws of victory. Are you going to end up with the magnificent seven or the dirty dozen? It's the campaign manager who makes the difference.

Michael lived in the electorate and had gone to school in Auckland Central. He was keen to make a contribution to the neighbourhood. My own background in politics is as a campaign organiser. I organised my first election campaign

OUT OF THE RED

Mike Gourley.

before I was legally able to vote. I had run numerous campaigns and thought I knew it all, but Michael Gourley introduced new techniques and new ways of organising our volunteer army that changed the way New Zealanders ran for office. The results were astonishing. In the 1981 election I received the biggest general seat majority in the country. This was a feat that had never been achieved by an Auckland Labour member of parliament since the legendary John A Lee. We did it again in 1984.

Michael did not have a background in politics. Yet here he was, outperforming the nation's most experienced political organisers. He was by profession a management consultant. That's a job description that covers a multitude of sins. The old joke that a consultant is a man who borrows your watch to tell you the time, was true. He had realised that companies mostly had the ideas to improve their businesses, but didn't know how to implement them.

Early in his career he'd fallen in with Human Synergistics. The company has surveyed over a million managers worldwide. Doing this many surveys means the results are statistically significant. (In social science it is very unusual to have been able to do surveys on this scale and this is why a lot of social science is more 'social' than 'science'.) What the company was looking for in these profiles was common factors that explain success and those that explain failure. They found them.

The secret indicator of success? It couldn't be simpler. It's how you think.

The secret indicator of success? It couldn't be simpler. It's how you think. It is your attitude, your beliefs and your values that influence your behaviour.

Just 15 per cent of individuals have an effective way of interpreting and reacting to the world. Those are the brutal statistics that come out of the million-sample survey. Eighty-five per cent of adults are not going to reach their potential success because they have an unsuccessful way of thinking.

By the 1960s, management psychologists had recognised from field surveys that successful people think in cause-and-effect terms. Successful people could see that if they did something it would have consequences. They believe their efforts make a difference. Doesn't everyone think like that? No. About 15 per cent of people think like that.

Most of the world's people think their efforts make no difference and that everything is the result of luck, chance or magic. (Have you bought a lottery ticket recently?)

Human Synergistics' achievement was to take this early work and refine it by doing

> Successful people think in cause-and-effect terms. Successful people could see that if they did something it would have consequences. They believe their efforts make a difference.

many thousands of organisational cultural surveys. Their research showed that all companies have one predominate culture, way of thinking, looking at and responding to the world. They found that individuals, organisations and whole countries could be described as having a predominant culture or way of thinking.

Each of us has a way of looking at the world. It's our personal culture. If you have an achievement culture, you will tend to succeed. If your primary culture is one of the non-achievement cultures, you will not reach your potential.

Now I hear you saying, 'that cannot be right, what about the environment?' Of course some people have greater advantages than others but resource cannot explain success. Some countries, like Singapore, have no resources and succeed, while countries with abundant resources, like Argentina, are basket-cases. Economists talk about 'the curse of oil'. And it's true that enormous natural wealth can produce some very perverse results.

Michael persuaded me to apply Human Synergistics techniques to my election campaign.

'To be more successful you must change the culture of your organisation,' he advised. I did not need much persuading that our culture was in need of change. The Auckland Central Labour Party was one of the oldest political organisations in the country and had witnessed some of the Labour Party's most

To be more successful you must change the culture of your organisation.

brutal internal feuds. The John A Lee expulsion was fought out inside the electorate. The party was secretive and combative. Loyalty was the highest virtue and dissent was treachery. Campaigns were organised by a small, exclusive coterie and volunteers were told what to do. It was inner city machine politics; tough and effective.

Professional politicians in the West are all democrats; but none of them trust democracy in their own campaigns. Democracy was a very nice theory, no doubt, but in practice totalitarian methods were considered more efficient. All political parties therefore set up campaign committees consisting of the candidate, the manager and as few people as possible. They were the generals and made all the decisions. The foot soldiers, the sloggers, the volunteers were just seen as pamphlet deliverers and expected to follow the orders, even when these were palpably absurd. Hence, cavalcades of cars driving through the town centre annoying everyone who sees them. I also remember Roger Douglas, bless him, launching the ACT party in Otara to persuade single mothers of the benefits of unrestrained capitalism (very few takers).

Michael turned the formula on its head and involved the volunteers in the campaign decisions. While a committee cannot write a pamphlet, all publicity was run past the volunteers. The tactics were openly discussed.

Michael told us, 'Secrecy does more harm to an organisation than any leak to the opposition.' So we laid out our total campaign strategy to the volunteers and invited their ideas. The result was not a novel campaign and in some ways it was very old fashioned.

In the 1980s, candidates gave up holding evening political

meetings. The voters preferred staying at home and watching the campaign on TV. Print media stopped covering such meetings and evening meetings are held too late to make it onto the six o'clock news. My volunteers wanted me to hold school-hall meetings in every neighbourhood. Even though these evening meetings were hard work and won me few votes, I agreed.

> **Secrecy does more harm to an organisation than any leak to the opposition.**

You cannot ask for volunteers' views and then ignore them. So, while the public meetings didn't win many votes, they gave a terrific shot in the arm to the volunteers. 'What we are really doing is changing the culture to one of mutual respect,' Michael Gourley said. The theory was that those who have a real say in the campaign work much harder for the candidate. The reality was: the biggest, most enthusiastic volunteer army in the country. And the result was the largest majority in the nation.

Desert survival

THE PARLIAMENTARY LABOUR caucus at the time was, the polite word is, dysfunctional. We were fighting like ferrets in a sack. A proposal would be praised or pilloried depending on whose proposal it was, irrespective of its intrinsic merits.

The party was so ideologically divided that we spent more time fighting each other than fighting Muldoon. Actually, we didn't spend any time fighting Muldoon. There was an open feud between the party activists in the country and the parliamentary wing. There were several open challenges to the leadership of then leader Bill Rowling, who had led us triumphantly to three crushing defeats. The mood in the British Labour Party at the time was, 'No compromise with the electorate!' I felt that there had to be a better way and asked Michael the question: 'Could Human Synergistics techniques work on an organisation like a parliamentary party?'

'Never tried a political party,' Michael replied, 'but our material will work with any type of organisation. It is an organisation, I take it?'

I thought we still just fitted that description but would be

DESERT SURVIVAL

unlikely to qualify in twelve months' time. 'We are going on a caucus retreat for three days to try to sort out our differences. Would you come?' I asked.

The caucus retreat is now famous in the annals of the Labour Party. It was held at Tatum Park, a scout holiday camp.

The Labour caucus is very secretive, very jealous of its exclusiveness. The only way anyone can attend a caucus meeting is to go through nine years of standing in unwinnable seats and get elected to parliament. Outsiders are very rarely admitted and then only to make some presentation after which they are expected to leave.

I said to the caucus I had proof that Michael was the rarest man in New Zealand politics; it was he, after all, who had produced parliament's biggest majority. My colleagues were as amazed as I was at my majority. The caucus allocated Michael the 'hangover slot' on Saturday morning to make a presentation. It was then that Michael had the caucus undertake 'the desert-survival exercise', that is possibly the most famous business game in the world. Human Synergistics developed it and many managers have done it, not knowing their copy is bootlegged.

The basis of the exercise is to imagine that as a group you are passengers on an aeroplane. The aeroplane has crashed in the desert. The pilot and co-pilot are dead. You have a map showing that the plane was off course and that the location of the nearest settlement is some kilometres away.

There is a list of some fifteen items that have survived the crash, ranging from a bottle of water to a revolver. First, each individual in the group must list the products in order of importance to survival. Then the group must put the items in order. As I recall the caucus was broken up into groups of seven.

When you do the exercise you quickly realise that the first question is whether to walk out or stay with the plane. As Michael explained to us, if you make the wrong decisions the experts say that, in the desert, with temperatures of up to 40° Celsius (104 degrees Fahrenheit), you will die. If you make the correct decisions you will survive.

The purpose of the exercise is to show people that collective decision-making in nearly every case outperforms the decision-making of the individual. When we added up our individual scores and compared them with the group scores, the average group score was higher than the average individual score and in many cases the group had outperformed any individual in the group.

What the exercise also showed was that within each group, there were individuals who knew the correct answer to each question. Yet in some groups, strong individuals persuaded the group to ignore the correct answer.

It is rather sobering to realise that if the exercise had been reality your ignoring a fellow passenger's advice would

DESERT SURVIVAL

David Lange, Michael Bassett, Roger Douglas and Mike Moore – the fish and chips brigade. (I had eaten my chips and gone.)
(*New Zealand Herald/APN*)

have got you all killed. It is even more of a reality check to discover that it was your false advice that would have killed everyone.

It is not the purpose of the desert-survival exercise to predict individual performance. Despite that, the exercise was remarkable in exposing real leadership. David Lange's group, which included Roger Douglas, would have lived. Shortly after this exercise, Lange was elected leader and went on to win the next election. He was a huge man, and weighed over twenty-eight stone before his stomach bypass (that is, more than 380 pounds or 170 kilograms). He took one look at the situation and said, 'I cannot walk,' and Roger Douglas, who was to become his finance minister, replied, 'Sure as hell, we are not carrying you.' A former minister of works put the revolver first on his list of resources (in case impatience got the better of him). One who had some minor medical knowledge put the salt tablets top (and died of thirst long before he'd have died of salt depletion). And Jim Anderton's group did walk out and all died. He later walked out of the Labour Government with very similar results.

The MPs who did best in the desert-survival exercise went on to become some of New Zealand's leading ministers in what is recognised as one of New Zealand's most remarkable governments.

The exercise is aimed at proving to groups that if they listen constructively rather than judgementally to what is being said, a group can solve even the toughest problem. It highlights the rational and interpersonal skills that are necessary to solve each problem.

We all know how destructive 'politics' are to our own business, organisation, sports club or any other group activity. Imagine how difficult it is to get people whose business is politics not to play politics with each other.

In just a few hours, the desert-survival exercise did more to persuade the Labour MPs to work together constructively than anything else we had ever tried. Commentators to this day cannot work out how a Labour Government, faced with the economic crisis of the 1980s, was so non-ideological in its response, and so willing to use economic techniques usually associated with conservative governments. Part of the answer is to be found at Tatum Park. The MPs learnt to examine situations in a constructive, non-judgemental way. To look for what worked. That's where it all started.

It is how you think

NEXT MICHAEL CIRCULATED Human Synergistics self-analysis questionnaires. The MPs had to answer a series of questions on carbonised paper. We then opened the sheets and found where we fitted in the personality/culture clock – a circle divided into segments numbered one to twelve. Each segment is a thinking style ranging from self-actualising to avoidance; achievement to dependent: humanistic-encouraging to oppositional; affiliative to power; perfectionist to conventional, and competitive to approving.

The results produced a buzz around the room. Most MPs were very thoughtful about what their results had shown. Although results were personal, a number of MPs showed me their own. I was impressed by how accurately the test had revealed information about the personalities of my colleagues – information it had taken me years to learn.

Michael explained that the healthiest styles are the constructive styles: achievement, self-actualising and affiliative. Organisations, whose members have this as their primary style, are very successful.

Key members of the caucus were delighted to learn that

> The healthiest styles are the constructive styles: achievement, self-actualising and affiliative. Organisations, whose members have this as their primary style, are very successful.

achievement was their primary style.

Not surprisingly, power was our secondary style.

A number of MPs had defensive styles, not daring to let anyone into their confidence. In a small minority of cases this was an imminently rational strategy for the characters concerned. Much more generally, it was a result of the caucus' paranoid culture. This rotten group culture we had allowed to develop dominated every individual in the group and was the single largest explanation of why we had been crushingly defeated three times in a row.

Michael Gourley was later to analyse the Cabinet's results. They were extraordinary. As a whole, the group was in the top 2 per cent of the million surveys that Human Synergistics had performed – and the top half of the group, including Lange/Douglas/Palmer/Moore was the best they'd seen. Ever. Anywhere. The individuals were almost pathologically achievement oriented. Gourley's achievement was to create a new culture in which those qualities could be expressed.

This first experience of the caucus began the process of dissolving the group's old attitudes. MPs were forced not

IT IS HOW YOU THINK

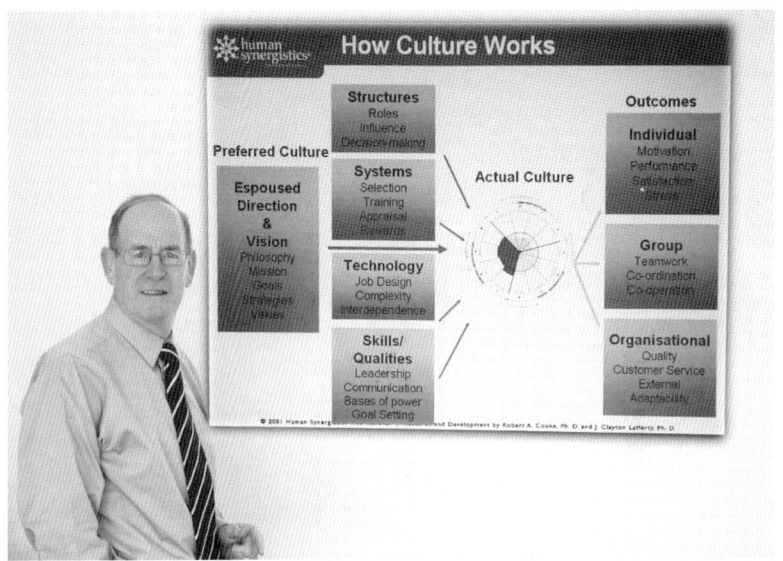

Mike Gourley with one of his culture charts.

only to re-evaluate one another's contribution, but also to examine their own conduct. The most negative MPs had the psychological shock of first having killed their group by refusing to listen to others and then having the questionnaire expose that their personal style was destructive.

Conversely, the majority of the caucus who had survived the desert and then found that their primary style was a positive one felt pretty good.

Everyone was left with plenty of things to think about.

> You can change your thinking and behaviour. Just being aware of negative traits is a start.

Michael emphasised that you can change your thinking and behaviour. Just being aware of negative traits is a start. The material gave advice on how to avoid defensive styles and how to develop a more constructive approach.

I went home from that retreat and carefully examined my chart. I asked the very small group who knew me best if it was accurate. I didn't altogether like what I heard but I accepted it must be true, and I made a determined effort to work on my weaknesses. And I'm not going to tell you what they were. Not until we know each other better. Let's move on.

Solutions are the problem

THE CAUCUS WAS so impressed that Michael was asked to stay on and facilitate our retreat. It was the first time that an outsider had ever been asked not just to attend a Labour caucus, but also to facilitate the discussion.

Over the next two days, the MPs used the lessons they had just learnt and were able to re-evaluate the way they had been acting. Decisions made at the retreat started a process that would result in the party's huge victory over the Muldoon Government. Even more significantly, the leading MPs learned to work together. It made us face up to the huge task we had in front of us when we did become government.

We were no more talented as individuals when we came out of Tatum Park. But as a group we had been transformed. We had found a way to work together constructively on very difficult problems; a way of empowering the group.

Let me give one small example. When caucus met, the agenda was a secret. No one knew what the chairman (our leader) would call for discussion. So we might spend an hour discussing the appointment of someone to lead a trade

Sir Robert Muldoon in parliament in a good mood.
(*Dominion Post Collection, Alexander Turnbull Library, Wellington, NZ, EP/1983/2952/6*)

delegation to Egypt and then find there were only twenty minutes left to discuss the privatisation of Telecom. After using Michael's techniques, we agreed that the agenda be published prior to the meeting. We were then able to scamper through the Egyptian appointment and spend more time on the big issues. Sounds simple? It probably is. But in those times, and in those circumstances, it was rocket science.

Michael facilitated discussion over how to combat Sir Robert Muldoon. In the previous three elections, Muldoon had completely destroyed us.

I recall that Michael's advice to us was not to debate alternative strategies but to concentrate on our analysis of what the problem was.

'Most organisations, when they have a problem, spend

SOLUTIONS ARE THE PROBLEM

far too little time examining the problem,' he told us. 'They jump straight into a debate on the two or three solutions that a proposition, an opposition and a synthesis produce. One of these solutions wins majority support and is implemented. But sooner or later it is realised that things haven't improved. So then the organisation goes back and re-examines the situation and finds that the solution didn't work because they'd identified the wrong problem.'

The problem we had identified was: How do we beat Muldoon? The real problem was: Why are we such a mess and how can we work together without trying to destroy our colleagues? We determined to ignore Muldoon and campaign by offering practical solutions to the real issues facing the nation. We set the agenda ourselves.

Michael got us to work nutting out new policy approaches on a number of issues; we were set in the same groups that we were in for the desert survival exercise. When an MP refused to listen to an opposing point of view it was sobering for him to be asked, 'And tell me again, Frank, why did you think we had to have a revolver?'

The Labour caucus had never worked in small groups. All discussions had been held in what was a mini-parliament, a hopeless way to make policy. Not only did our small groups work together well, but also, when we reported back, we found widespread consensus on issues we had previously been hopelessly divided on.

When we became government and found a major crisis in the economy, the techniques we had learnt at Tatum Park enabled us to work though the issues and transform the country.

Today in New Zealand no one, not even the Left, advocates import controls, subsidies for farming and centralised wage controls, but removing them had been regarded as politically impossible. It was, you might think, a very peculiar country in those days. And that's true. The prevailing climate of ideas was so strong that things happened then that would never be tolerated now. Do you remember that margarine was a controlled substance? You could use it for medicinal purposes but you had to have a doctor's prescription. We were a butter-producing country, you see, and margarine was the enemy of the 'kiwi way'. Of course, this couldn't happen today.

But having said that, in thirty years people may be scratching their heads saying, 'You know, at the turn of the century it was illegal for an employer to talk to his employees about their wages. He'd be taken to a tribunal and fined.'

Achievement thinking still has a role to play; arguably we need it more than ever. After our seven 'fat years' we might want to be thinking about the future a little more robustly.

The achieving society

TATUM PARK WAS a revelation to me. How had Michael managed to get such a warring group to work together? I wanted to know what the research basis was of the techniques that Human Synergistics was using.

Michael introduced me to the work of Professor David McClelland and lent me his book, *The Achieving Society*.* I was in hospital at the time so perhaps I was vulnerable to suggestion. The blurb for the book says:

'Applying the methods of the behavioural sciences, this book provides a factual basis for evaluating theories – economic, historical, and sociological – that explain the rise and fall of civilisations.'

This is an intriguing subject. There have been thousands of books written on why civilisations rise and fall.

What David McClelland did was to take his research on achievement and to see if it applied to nations. Do nations succeed when achievement thinking becomes the nation's thinking style?

---

* David McClelland, *The Achieving Society* (New York: Free Press, 1961)

This is what he says about achievers: 'All such people have certain values: the principle one is that they believe that their efforts do make a difference. They believe that what they do, therefore, is important, that their contribution has value. They believe in cause and effect, that what they individually do has results that are measurable and important.'

McClelland then asked the question: is the real reason that some societies are more successful than others because the culture of those societies is achievement orientated?

He then made the assumption that what we teach our children reflects our society's core values. Nursery rhymes and children's stories have proved to be well-preserved. He had his senior students analyse the language of children's stories and nursery rhymes to determine their achievement values. He then looked to see if there was a correlation between the achievement values in the education curriculum and the achievement of the nation. There is an astonishing correlation.

'Aladdin' is an example of a story that has no achievement values. Everything that happens to Aladdin is the result of luck, chance and magic. The Arabs had developed a

Professor David McClelland.

remarkable civilisation that stretched to Spain, yet Arabia at the time the story came into being was in decline.

An example of a very high achievement story is 'Dick Whittington'. Dick Whittington is the boy who by his wits becomes the lord mayor of London. There is no chance or magic in his story. At the time this story became most popular (the first pantomime of it was produced in the early nineteenth century) Britain was the wealthiest and most powerful nation on earth.

I am personally convinced that it is the values of an individual, a business, an organisation and a nation that determine success. Too many individuals, businesses, organisations and nations have what I call a lotto culture. They believe their efforts make no difference and success is just a matter of fate.

> It is the values of an individual, a business, an organisation and a nation that determine success.

I found Professor McClelland's book remarkable and persuasive. It was also very sobering, as he had done an analysis of modern school books. He had analysed the school textbooks of a large number of nations, including New Zealand's. McClelland found that 'to a remarkable extent our achievement levels in children's readers forecast which countries will do well or poorly'.

In 1950, after studying the school books of war-damaged Japan he wrote, 'One would predict that the achievement level of Japanese will rise over the years as these boys grow into maturity, and also that Japan will move from a state of "under-achievement" in the economic sphere to that of an "overachiever", say by 1970.' In 1950 this was the prediction least likely to come true.

He found that New Zealand textbooks in the 1930s were amongst those that had the highest achievement values. In the 1950s New Zealand enjoyed one of the world's highest standards of living.

But after examining New Zealand school readers post-war, McClelland placed New Zealand at the top of the underachievers – a reasonable description of our economic performance from 1960 to 1980.

So I regret to say, the popularity of Harry Potter is not entirely comforting, even for those who value the sheer fact of children reading books.

Clay Lafferty

THE ACHIEVEMENT OF Dr Clay Lafferty was to refine the work of David McClelland and give it a practical application. If it applied to businesses and to nations, it was something individuals, organisations and governments could utilise in making strategic decisions. By doing hundreds of thousands of surveys, Lafferty discovered that he could refine the achievement style. Interestingly, he found that the most successful style was not, as McClelland thought, 'achievement' but 'self-actualising'. Self-actualising people are rounded individuals who are able to measure their achievements in their own terms; who are satisfied with their own success.

On a visit to the United States I travelled to Harvard University to meet Professor McClelland. He had a foundation. I met his associates and spent a fascinating day discussing his research. But I did not meet the guru. He had become fascinated with the concept of happiness and had found to his surprise that while achievement people were happier than those whose styles were negative, the most contented people he had found were Buddhist monks in Thailand.

Professor McClelland had gone off to Mexico to measure the profile of some Catholic nuns to see if they were also content.

I did not find that this knowledge made me want to abandon the world for a monastery and I think Lafferty's discovery of the self-actualised style, as being the most fulfilling, is the answer.

I met Dr Lafferty when he visited New Zealand in the nineties. I recall I asked him if people's concept of time was a predictor of success. I had found that how people think about time was very revealing. The go-getters so often have their watches set five minutes fast.

He asked me how I saw time. 'Like a fast moving train that never stops,' I said. He said he was not surprised at my answer and told me many people see time as slow moving clouds.

He then asked me to draw time as three circles. One circle for the past, a second for the present and a third circle for the future. You might like to try it.

> The most successful style was not, as McClelland thought, 'achievement' but 'self-actualising'. Self-actualising people are rounded individuals who are able to measure their achievements in their own terms; who are satisfied with their own success.

Clay Lafferty and me on his trip to New Zealand.

I drew a small circle for the past, a bigger circle for the present and a third, larger circle for the future.

My wife also drew three circles, all about the same size and overlapping.

Clay told me that my circles showed a man who ought to slow down a bit and enjoy the present. I should reflect that the past does impact on the future.

In contrast he said that my wife's overlapping circles showed a very balanced perspective and an understanding that our past, present and future all overlap.

A number of businessmen who are fans of his work held a dinner for Clay and his wife. After dinner we got him to speak about his latest research. He said that he felt they were close to proving that an organisation's culture was the key to its success. How true this is. Starbucks proclaims that its single greatest asset and competitive advantage is its staff. By contrast, Enron treated its staff so badly that managers were required to fire the bottom 10 per cent of workers every year – whether they'd performed poorly or well. Their respective cultures led precisely to the outcomes we are familiar with.

So much for the theory

AFTER NINE YEARS of a National Government behaving like a socialist one (and remember that national socialism is not a road a country should go down) the country voted in what came to be known as the Lange/Douglas Government. Bliss it was in that dawn to be alive. The feeling lasted roughly until morning tea . . .

I found myself in government in the middle of the most serious financial crisis in our history. There had been a run on the kiwi dollar and all of the government's reserves had gone. The Reserve Bank had suspended all foreign exchange dealings on the Sunday after the election. Our lines of credit had been exhausted and the government could not meet the next payment on an overseas loan. Default on one loan and it is a default on all loans. The country was just a few days from default. We were faced with calling in the International Monetary Fund (IMF) or making the hard decisions ourselves. There was no way we were going to hand over sovereignty to the IMF. The cabinet determined to tackle the problems.

On that Sunday after the election, officials travelled to Auckland to give David Lange a briefing, to advise why the

SO MUCH FOR THE THEORY

David Lange taking a call from Sir Robert Muldoon, election night, 1984. He had no idea of the financial problems we had just inherited. (*New Zealand Herald/APN*)

Reserve Bank had had to suspend foreign exchange dealing and to deliver a massive document from Treasury on the economic crisis. David called me around to his home that afternoon and said that the officials had advised the crisis was very serious. He gave me a copy of the Treasury briefing and asked me to give him my views in the morning. I took it home and began reading. Even though it was a government document, I could not put it down. I was still reading it at 3 a.m.

These Treasury mandarins are the cream of the civil service. They pride themselves on clear thinking and a lucid prose style. They are highly intelligent, highly educated, and for the previous nine years – as Robert Muldoon had been managing the economy – they had been very underemployed. They'd had the time and the energy to compile this dossier, which was the most comprehensive analysis of economic basket weaving you could ever have hoped to read.

I had gone though a campaign criticising the government's economic management in what I had thought were colourful terms. I discovered that I had understated the situation. As I read each economic problem, I thought of a political solution. Then as I read the next problem, I realised my political solution was making things worse rather than better. This went on hour after hour. The Treasury analysis was implacable.

At three in the morning I put down the briefing documents and surveyed the wreckage for an hour. What a picture it was. Agriculture had been receiving massive subsidies through Muldoon's mechanism: Supplementary Minimum Prices. You could see how it had happened. The price of sheep meat had collapsed for a while in the 1970s (it happens now and again). The farmers had gone to Muldoon saying, 'We can't make ends meet, and it's the government's fault. Our costs are high because you've put these tariffs on everything from machinery to gumboots. Transport is twice the price it should be because of your regulations, and the freezing works and the wharves are the most inefficient in Australasia because you've caved in to the wharfies every time they threaten to strike. Now our incomes have collapsed, and these costs you've imposed on us are going to put us out of business. You don't want that because we're 60 per cent of the country's export earnings. It's your problem, you fix it.'

SO MUCH FOR THE THEORY

Muldoon's fix was a subsidy. And the one-way ratchet went round another notch. It was all so interconnected, so interdependent that you couldn't reform any single part of the system. But it couldn't go on, because apart from the immediate cash problems, our subsidies were being met with countervailing tariffs in America and Europe. Our markets were turning their backs on us. We were facing an issue of national survival.

I realised that the measures we would have to take would be both radical and unpopular. This mess was so comprehensive I couldn't see any way our government could be re-elected. The worst thing was this: we were going to carry the can for nine years of Muldoon's manias. He had brought the country to the edge of bankruptcy and we were going to be the ones to get the blame for the bankruptcy itself. Nothing could better confirm Labour's reputation for economic mismanagement! What a trap the old tusker had set for us! And there we were, at 4 a.m. – the hour before dawn – the darkest hour of the night, deep in it.

If we are going to be defeated, let us at least be defeated doing what is best for the country. With that thought I went to sleep.

In the morning I found that other ministers had reached the same conclusion. This is the reason the Lange Labour Government was more free enterprise than Margaret Thatcher. We weren't trying to be re-elected – but just trying to make quality decisions.

We knew that New Zealand's centralised controlled economy had collapsed and there was no other choice than to deregulate.

OUT OF THE RED

Me, Roger Douglas and David Caygill. All smiles as we try to fix the economy. (*Dominion Post*)

I became one of the finance ministers; 'the troika': Roger Douglas, the architect, me, who might be described as the man with the tool kit and the welding gear, and David Caygill, the much under-valued minister of trade and industry who, very quietly and to the world's general astonishment, dismantled the nation's Byzantine system of price controls.

There we were. It was like the early scenes of a disaster movie with things going very badly but with the capacity to go, very quickly, very much worse. The international markets knew something of our troubles and were betting against the dollar. We devalued the currency by 20 per cent. The kiwi rallied. Six months later we floated the dollar and the statutory marketing boards that felt it would slump got very badly burnt in their currency speculations.

The scale of our task had been made apparent to us by Treasury; now we had to make it apparent to the country. We knew we could not achieve change unless we took the nation with us. The pre-Tatum Park mindset might have tempted us to act first and then inform the country of the reasons for our actions. The achievement thought was – and I can only hint at how the civil service opposed the idea – to publish all the briefing documents that had been supplied to the incoming government.

Today, all new governments release these documents and the civil service write them knowing their advice will be made public. That's why they are not very interesting. In those days, the government was so secretive that the officials allowed themselves to be very frank.

The book was a best seller. Muldoon's own cabinet colleagues read with astonishment the things that Muldoon had kept from them. Jim McLay confessed he had had no idea how bad things were.

The effect of publication was palpable. A large part of New Zealand realised they were being taken into the government's confidence.

It wasn't welcomed by everyone, of course. We invited a cross-section of the nation to discuss the crisis. A summit meeting was held in parliament. We asked a number of academics to chair the conference. They could see the risk that such an opportunity presented and every last one of them declined.

Sir Ron Trotter.

Then we asked Sir Ron Trotter, chairman of New Zealand's largest firm. He had enormous reputational capital. He risked it. He accepted immediately.

Sir Ron was superb. Not just in chairing the summit but then in rallying business to support what were painful reforms. Sir Ron is a patriot. He later played a crucial role in the success of the SOE reforms. I was to ask him to take the position of chairman of the SOE advisory committee or chairman of Telecom. I said I needed him in both jobs but no one could do both. I think I offended him and he accepted both.

Telecom's success is well documented but he taught this politician with no business experience many valuable lessons. One is that there is no excuse for failure. Did the Gulf War put pressures on budgets? 'There's always a Gulf War!' he'd say. There's always a reason why forecasts are threatened. But that's no reason for targets not being met. There is no point in setting goals unless everyone understands they must be met. Sir Ron, even though he was recognised by his peers as New Zealand's captain of industry, is not a wealthy man. As an employee he had to give up income to work for the government at the nominal

> 'There's always a Gulf War!' he'd say. There's always a reason why forecasts are threatened. But that's no reason for targets not being met.

rates we paid. Other leading businessmen who accepted appointment to boards also made considerable financial sacrifices to serve their country. Their leadership was crucial and their remarkable contribution to their nation has never been properly acknowledged.

I would like to say that my speech to the summit was great but I cannot prove it. The cameraman was so interested that he forgot to put any film in the camera. Or so he said. I accepted his excuse. Yes, I had a lot to learn.

The conference called on the government to make radical changes. The federation of farmers called for the end of agricultural subsidies; the manufacturers – for the abolition of import protection; the bankers – for financial deregulation. Even the trade union movement said there had to be change from centralised wage controls to free wage bargaining. There was a sense of unanimity that was astonishing. A sense of growth, of optimism, that there was indeed a better way if we took the tough decisions. And the greatest unanimity was on the most important point. Everyone agreed: 'Don't start with me.'

But we had made the first steps towards real reform. We had an acceptance that there had to be change, and that we had a vision of how the country could be better. The government began a programme that came to be called Rogernomics after the finance minister Sir Roger Douglas. Import licensing was abolished, tariffs cut, agricultural subsidies removed, financial regulations repealed and the dollar was floated. Income tax was cut from sixty-six cents to thirty-three cents per dollar and a broad-based goods and services tax (GST) was introduced. We removed price controls and ended government-controlled wage fixing.

To our surprise the tougher the decisions we made, the more popular we became. I soon found myself tackling the intractable problems of the railways. A real test for Human Synergistic theories.

Saving rail

I HAD LED a big campaign to 'Save Rail' against the previous government's attempts to reform the railway. Everyone knew New Zealand Rail was in need of reform. I thought the previous government actually believed rail could not be saved and its reforms were really designed to allow railways to fade away and let all freight go by road.

In my book *I've Been Thinking*, I have written stories about the mess the rail service was in. There is the one about the farmer and his tractor. I'd been minister of railways for only a matter of days when my office presented me with a letter to sign. A farmer had written in to say that New Zealand Rail could not find his tractor. The letter informed him that he could apply for compensation but the limit was a hundred dollars per package and a tractor was one package.

'I cannot sign a letter saying, "We can't find your tractor but you can have a hundred dollars".'

'Minister, we have searched extensively for it. The tractor cannot be found.'

There was good news. When they rang the farmer he said he'd found it. He came, as I recall, from the middle of the

SAVING RAIL

I campaigned on the 'Save Rail' train throughout New Zealand. (*Courtesy of Graeme McClare*)

Peter Neilson, Koro Wetere, Colin Moyle, Peter Tapsell, Bob Tizard, Michael Bassett, Bruce Gregory. I persuaded the Labour caucus members to support my 'Save Rail' campaign and take the train to the Tatum Park retreat. (*Dominion Post Collection, Alexander Turnbull Library, Wellington, NZ, H-102-013*)

> The moral of the story, as I said, is that one man with the correct incentives can outperform twenty-two thousand railway employees who have none.

North Island. He had driven his car to Auckland and then followed the main trunk line for hundreds of kilometres. He took his car in the rail ferry to Picton where he found his tractor sitting on a siding. It had not been unloaded at its destination and had travelled in error across Cook Strait. No one had got around to sending it back.

The moral of the story, as I said, is that one man with the correct incentives can outperform twenty-two thousand railway employees who have none. He had the values necessary for tractor-finding. These values included (but weren't limited to) the fact that he owned it, he needed it, he wanted it.

My staff told me that losing a tractor was nothing. Once the railways had lost a whole train of export frozen lamb. 'We only found the train when members of the public rang up asking what the awful smell was.'

As a new minister I decided that I should at least make a visit to the railways head office, which was situated above the Wellington railway station.

'There are over a thousand employees in head office,' I was told. 'It will take you days to make a visit and you don't have the time.'

'Very well, I will visit a floor a day,' I said.

Apparently no minister in the institutional memory of the department had ever visited head office. What I found shocked me. Staff were working in Victorian conditions. I recall visiting one massive office and there were around twenty people counting and checking piles of paper.

'What are these people doing?' I asked.

'They are counting the number of railway passenger tickets sold on the Wellington suburban rail system,' was the answer.

'Why do you do that? Why not simply audit tickets by way of a sample?' I asked.

A few days later I received the answer. It was a memo signed by the general manager advising me that in the 1960s an MP had asked in parliament how many tickets and to what value had been issued on the Johnsonville line the previous Monday. Railways had been unable to answer. Since then, each day, all passenger tickets had been counted and the value recorded, just in case some MP asked that question again. No MP had.

I told them that they could stop. If the question was asked again in parliament I undertook to get up and say that I didn't know.

New Zealand Rail was losing one million dollars a day. The National Government had made the railways a corporation and had appointed directors from the private sector to the board. The new board, faced with what seemed to be intractable problems and a management that had a public-sector mentality, had appointed the famous American firm of consultants Booz Allen Hamilton (Booz Allen). They were commissioned to write a report, which had been delivered to New Zealand Rail shortly before the election.

All this was publicly known. The rail unions had pressed me prior to the election to announce a resumption of the distance restriction on the movement of freight. By law all freight moving more than fifty miles (eighty kilometres) used to have to go by rail. The previous government, in an almost libertarian spasm, had lifted the restriction. I told the unions that it was quite impossible to reinstate it.

The unions also asked me to publicly announce that the incoming government would ditch the Booz Allen report. Again I declined saying that I could not reject a report that I had not read. What I would do was make the report's findings public.

On becoming minister I discovered that the management of the railways was even more hostile than the unions to the Booz Allen report and was trying to bury it in further reports. There was a reason for that, as I was to find out. It was cultural.

In my incoming briefing from New Zealand Rail was a depressing list of problems and no solutions. My first contact with the general manager was to ask him how railways would be affected by the 20 per cent devaluation. I had already asked this question of Air New Zealand to be told that the then general manager of the airline, Norman Geary, had been telephoned at home at one in the morning to be advised that the prime minister had called a general election. His instruction was to contact London and obtain forward cover against the New Zealand dollar. This he achieved by 4 a.m. Air New Zealand had no losses. The shipping corporation had waited two weeks before seeking foreign exchange cover and had lost twelve million dollars.

When I asked if New Zealand Rail had any forward cover, I was informed that railways had all sorts of covers and tarpaulins but what was a forward cover? I explained that forward cover was to protect against a change in the value of the currency.

'Why does New Zealand Rail need to protect itself against a currency change?' the general manager asked.

I paused to look at him a little more intently and then said, 'You have a major civil engineering project, the main trunk line electrification project, which must be paid for in Japanese yen. It is now 20 per cent more expensive than it was a week ago.'

'But surely the Treasury will compensate us for that,' he said.

'But surely it will not.' I told him New Zealand Rail was now a corporation and this was a treasury risk that it was expected to plan for. It hadn't. Indeed I found it didn't have a treasury.

So the result of my first briefing was to inform New Zealand Rail's general manager that his corporation had lost another sixty million dollars. He did not seem as upset as I would have been to discover I had lost sixty million dollars. Perhaps he saw it as the natural price of sixty days in office.

Excellent as it was in other areas, the Treasury briefing on the railways was of no practical assistance. It was clear they thought that the organisation was a hopeless basket-case. Their only advice was to split off the profitable rail ferries between the North and South Islands into a separate business.

The Treasury persisted with this piece of useless advice the whole time that I was minister. The officials refused to look at the impact this would have upon railways. If New Zealand Rail couldn't run the rail ferries, it couldn't control its network timetable.

I met with the chairman of the railways board, Lindsay Paps. He was a successful corporate lawyer who had become a director of a large number of companies – from memory, over twenty. I asked him what his strategy was.

'We can't compete with the trucking industry that is attacking our business, except by price,' he said. 'I have instructed railways to keep cutting prices to retain the business. We will go on cutting prices until we have won back our market share.'

Mr Paps saw – not unreasonably – that he could keep cutting prices indefinitely because the taxpayer would end up paying (and more than once). As a finance minister facing a multi-billion dollar deficit and demands for more spending on education and health, I thought we needed a different solution.

As a Labour Party minister I also spoke with the rail unions. The national union of railwaymen (NUR), wanted New Zealand Rail to again be a government department, long-distance freight to be regulated and the 'service' subsidised. Their answer was also the taxpayer.

I received sensible advice from just two sources.

There was a different union representing the locomotive drivers. The secretary of the union was Dick Williams. He should be Sir Richard for what he did then, but not everyone gets what they deserve in life. As much as anyone in the government or the management, that union secretary saved rail for New Zealand.

'If you want to save rail, Richard, you must reduce costs. We need to go to one-man trains. We have a plan to implement this.'

This astonished me. A trade union secretary advocating reducing staff to achieve a productivity improvement! That wasn't in the textbook on industrial relations.

I said to him. 'This proposal will halve the number of jobs for your members.'

He replied 'If there is no New Zealand Rail there will be no jobs for any of my members. We know that there are now one-man trains in Australia and in the United States. Their safety record is slightly better than ours. One-man trains are coming. Without them you cannot compete with trucks.'

Everything he said was true. He'd faced up to the situation in a way no one else had dared to. New Zealand trains had three men because that was the number that trains had always had. Steam trains needed a driver and a stoker to keep the fire going. The guard at the back, who in the United States was more accurately called the brakeman, was there to apply the brakes.

The stoker had been redundant since the introduction of diesel trains. The guards on trains had been redundant since the early 1960s when automatic brakes had been introduced. The unions had insisted the positions remain, so now three men ran every train, two of whom contributed nothing. It was thought to be a victory for the working man.

I was puzzled as to why it was the union and not the management that was bringing me this advice. So I pressed the union secretary as to why the union's thinking was so constructive.

He asked me if I remembered the series of train crashes and derailments a few years earlier. 'Our members,' he said, 'were under a lot of pressure.' Drivers were being killed and those that survived had to endure inquiries that invariably found them at fault. The union believed that the system was unsafe. The management disagreed. The train crashes had generated very bad publicity, so when the union came up with a proposal for a safety programme for the engine drivers, management agreed to fund it.

The union chose Human Synergistics to develop a safety programme. The training had been a huge success. Where previously there had been a rail crash a month, following the training there had not been a crash for over a year.

Human Synergistics had approached the problem of rail crashes in a completely innovative way.

Railways had taught engine drivers by lectures and exams. The problem with lectures is that students do not pick up everything that the lecturer says. The problem with exams is that the pass mark had been 70 per cent. That leaves a 30 per cent gap in the driver's knowledge.

An engine driver operating a four-hundred-tonne train travelling at eighty kilometres an hour needs to know not 70 per cent of his craft, but 100 per cent. Human Synergistics realised that nearly half of all the locomotive drivers could not accurately interpret all of the railway signals. Not knowing what the rail signal means is pretty scary.

Human Synergistics introduced a training scheme based on the principle that adults learn from experience. They found the engine drivers who had been in dangerous situations (for example, having to stop, knowing another train was coming up behind) could describe not only how they warned of the stoppage but also how they felt. The drivers taught each other.

> **Adults learn from experience.**

The union's secretary said his members were so impressed with the safety programme that the union decided to ask Human Synergistics to work with them on other issues that the union faced.

'When we started to work on problems in this way we couldn't stop. We realised that unless there were fundamental changes the organisation wouldn't actually survive. If rail went so did our jobs. So we started to see what we could do to make a rail system competitive. It was easy to see that one-man trains hauling forty wagons have got to be more competitive than the same train with two extra staff also pulling around a twenty-tonne guard van. We could see that management sooner or later would propose one-man trains. Either we could have it imposed on us or we could work co-operatively to set up a system that's in the best interests of our members.'

When I tackled management about one-man trains, they at first denied they were working on it. (I think they thought that I would be opposed to the reduction in staff.) Then management told me the locomotive engine drivers would never accept it. They were stunned when I said that the locomotive engine drivers union had not only advocated it but had produced a plan. 'Here it is.'

When my staff studied the drivers' plan, we saw that in spite of its merits, it was very unfair to the NUR who represented the guards. One of the problems of the railway system was that it was class ridden. The locomotive engine drivers looked down on the guards. The office staff looked down on those working in the yard. The management looked down on – and had no contact with – anyone except themselves. Railways had a class system so rigid it was almost medieval. An employee who joined as a guard could never become a driver. The problem with the engine drivers' plan, the management's and indeed the guards', was that none of them allowed for the revolutionary idea of a guard becoming a driver. It was a caste system, almost (the untouchables were the passengers).

You think I exaggerate? As part of my desire as minister to inspect the railways, I said to the general manager one day that I intended to go down to the rail yard to view the rail ferry being loaded at night. There was some safety issue and I wanted to go and see for myself. The general manager tried to talk me out of it.

It was only when he saw that I was determined that he admitted the control of the unions was so strong, that if any member of the management stepped into the rail yards, work would stop.

'Well I am going tonight and you are coming with me. You'll be okay.' I said. 'I'll show you how a politician visits a worksite.' I rang the union secretary and said that I was going to look at the problem that night and would he like to come? I did not mention I was also bringing the general manager. When we all met, the union secretary could not bring himself to say to me that if the manager stepped on the yard all work would stop. After the workers got over the shock of seeing, at midnight, the minister, the union secretary, the general manager and the stationmaster inspecting the shunting operation, they were pleased to see us. It was something the general manager had never witnessed. I saw a pothole that needed filling. I turned to the stationmaster, who was also banned by the union, and said, 'This is unsafe. I want it filled tomorrow. I want you to personally inspect it tomorrow night and report to me that it is fixed. From now on I want you to personally inspect that conditions are safe.' The men were delighted but so was the stationmaster who could now walk onto his own rail yard.

Railways today is an organisation that promotes on merit and staff are trained to be multi-skilled. The railways experience shows that New Zealanders can slip into accepting class differences but with leadership we can also be egalitarian and promote on merit. I have been impressed with how inspiring it is to work in a firm like Mainfreight where there are managers who started as loaders, and where each person on the staff knows they can rise to the top by their own efforts.

Managers should always be looking for talent to promote. Karen Smith decided to take a job as a waitress in parliament when her children were school age. Her personality was such that parliamentary services offered her a job as receptionist on the ground floor of the building where ACT MPs had their office. When we needed a receptionist, Ken Shirley, ACT's deputy leader, said, 'Why don't we employ that friendly woman on the ground floor?' Karen had never worked in an office, had left school without qualifications, but she was willing to learn. She not only mastered keyboard skills but also became so proficient on the computer she was soon in charge of up to twenty temporary staff. When other parties said to her, 'Why is a Maori working for ACT?' she replied, 'Because they gave me the opportunity.' When her husband took a job in Auckland, ACT offered her a position in head office. Within a year she was party manager. In the old New Zealand Rail she would have still been a waitress.

It was not just the stationmasters who were stuck in their offices. Management was by processing paper rather than by action. One day the general manager showed me plans for a new rail yard in a South Island provincial town.

'Isn't the railway station on the other side of the yard?' I asked. I then realised that the management had never been to this railway yard and the plan had been mirror reversed.

Here's the rule: whenever possible, go look yourself. It is obvious that people do not report. Take a camera. A photo speaks volumes about what you did and did not like.

I recall my first visit to Samoa. Having carefully read all the briefing documents, I'd been surprised to see how many cars Samoa imports from the United States. The moment I arrived I saw the answer. In Samoa they drive on the right-hand side of the road. A fact left out of every briefing document.

I'm not a great believer in surprise visits. The advantage of announcing that you are coming gives the organisation time to put on its best performance. It is often very sobering to realise what some organisations regard as their best. You can calculate that everyone else would be receiving a service level considerably lower.

I got good advice from another source. It was from the late Malcolm McConnell, the founder of McConnell Dowell, the civil engineering firm. He had been appointed a director of the railways corporation. Malcolm contacted me to say that as the previous government had appointed him he was willing to resign and allow me to appoint a person of my choice. What he would like to do was give me his frank advice. I invited him to do so.

He told me that the management of the corporation was hopeless. The senior managers had opposed every attempt to introduce businesslike practices. It had been his idea to commission the Booz Allen report because the board just had to have some alternative advice.

He also said he thought that the Booz Allen report was an important document but it contained no advice as to how to implement its suggestions. 'What you need is a new general manager from the private sector.'

He had put his finger right on it. Malcolm McConnell became the only director I kept on and we became great friends. When I received my copy of the Booz Allen report I found it was a devastating critique of New Zealand Rail. In its hundreds of pages it contains valuable information as to what railways had to be in order to be competitive. What the report did not contain was how to achieve this.

I had to turn to Human Synergistics.

Implementing change

I SOUGHT ADVICE from my friend Michael Gourley. I gave him a copy of the Booz Allen report. 'What would Human Synergistics recommend?'

Michael pointed out to me that the report often described management's plans, (Booz Allen had found the management plan for one-man trains) and the report frequently said, 'We find management's plans to be sound.' 'This means,' he said, 'there is talent inside the railways. They know the answers to most of the issues they face. What they don't know is how to introduce fundamental change successfully.'

'You cannot change any organisation or individual until that organisation or individual accepts change is needed,' said Michael. 'The Booz Allen report gives us an opportunity to have

> You cannot change any organisation or individual until that organisation or individual accepts change is needed.

management and employees face the reality that change is not an option, it is the only choice.'

I then said to him 'What I would like to do is organise a railway summit in parliament. I want to invite the board, the senior management and a cross-section of the staff, including the unions. I have given an undertaking to the unions to reveal the content of the Booz Allen report. I proposed to do so at the summit. Could you help facilitate such a gathering?'

Michael said that he had never facilitated anything as large as what I was proposing. He consulted with colleagues. They thought there were some significant risks but it could be done.

I then rang up Chuck Hoppe, the vice-president of Booz Allen in Washington DC and told him that he was coming to New Zealand to present the report, not just to the board and management but also to a cross-section of the employees and the unions. He told me that he had never done such a presentation and had very grave doubts about its wisdom.

He wasn't the only one. Two-thirds of the conference consisted of the country's most feared trade unionists. Management was petrified that the conference would be hi-jacked.

The engine drivers union immediately agreed to come. The management and board were horrified but had no choice. The NUR said that they did not need to read the Booz Allen report to know they were totally opposed and they would not come.

I made every effort to persuade them. I knew the chairman, Finlayson, well. He was in charge of catering at the

Christchurch railway station. So when visiting Christchurch I called in and told him to come with me. I took him in my ministerial car and tried to persuade him to change his mind. He wouldn't. I was going to fly in a small government plane to Blenheim. I dismissed my car and said, 'Get in. We need to talk. The plane can take you back.' He was reluctant and I virtually kidnapped him. It was all to no avail. I could hardly get him to say anything on the aeroplane. I subsequently found out that Finlayson was petrified of flying and he thought that I'd taken him by plane believing that would make him agree to anything. It was the end of my friendship with the NUR.

The railway summit was unique. Some 350 employees and members of management gathered in the legislative chamber of parliament. The chamber was packed. There was the electric atmosphere of an expectant crowd. This was history in the making. And it was true, what happened that day was probably as important, if not more, as most of the legislation that had gone through the place when it had been the upper house.

I opened the conference with a short speech pointing out how important an efficient railway network is to the nation. I stated that my goal was to create the most efficient and effective narrow-gauge railway in the world. I was personally committed to it and could see no reason why together we could not achieve it. I then introduced Chuck Hoppe to do the heavy lifting. He's a big fellow, Chuck, with a big American voice.

He gave a brilliant presentation. There wasn't a sound to be heard as he spoke. He was talking about their livelihood.

Many rail employees work for the railways because they have a passion for rail. He was explaining their business in clearer terms than they had ever heard before. It was a devastating indictment, in fact, of years of mismanagement. There was a moment when he finished speaking and then a long, long round of applause.

Obviously it hadn't been as much of a risk as we'd all thought. These things are more apparent in hindsight. Twelve months before the election I had travelled to the United States on an American Government visitor programme. These programmes are excellent. The United States Government allows visitors to go and see whatever they like. I had asked the general manager of New Zealand Rail, just before he was about to appear in front of a parliamentary select committee of which I was a senior opposition member, whether I could visit Booz Allen. Would he arrange it? Given the choice between a three-hour public grilling or arranging an introduction, he said yes.

I was given Chuck's number at work. I arrived in Washington and checked into my hotel. I had an appointment the next day with an official from the department of agriculture who was to facilitate my visit. (It was assumed that as I was from New Zealand I was interested in farms.)

I telephoned Booz Allen and found that Chuck was delighted to hear from me. He said why didn't I come over? He gave me the instructions for the taxi driver and said, 'Bring your passport.'

It wasn't a joke about Maryland. The passport was for security against lawsuits. Booz Allen is such a big firm of consultants that often their clients have conflicts of interest. The security was part of their Chinese walls. 'Whenever we are sued,' which I took was often, 'we just take the jury though a tour. It never fails to impress.' I am still impressed twenty years later. While the transport section of the firm had dozens of staff, it was only a small part of the firm and rail a smaller section still.

Despite that, Booz Allen was the world's largest rail consultancy. We started talking trains. In the next three hours I learnt more about railways than I had learnt as opposition spokesman in three years.

Chuck explained that trucks outperform trains on all distances under five hundred miles (800 km). The longest train trip in New Zealand is four hundred miles (640 km). This is why rail ferries are crucial; they convert rail journeys into six hundred miles (970 km).

Rail's advantage over trucks is that one locomotive can haul a hundred wagons. But New Zealand trains were short, usually less than twenty wagons plus the guard's van, which was often the heaviest wagon.

The complexity of running a railway could be measured by the number of 'heads'. Heads occur when two trains meet and have to pass. New Zealand has a single-track railway. Every twenty-four hours there were over 120 heads on the main trunk line. This meant the New Zealand railway needed a very elaborate signal system. Booz Allen had done a computer simulation of the New Zealand railway and if it used longer trains the system could run with as little as twelve heads per day.

'So you could de-signal the line and save millions a year. The drivers could be given two-way radios and arrange between them where they will pass. It's very safe as train drivers have a thing about not liking to crash.'

Chuck not only knew about trains, he knew a lot about transport. He taught me, that day, what I have never seen in a textbook, and what I call 'Hoppe's law of network economics'.

'If you introduce competition to a network, the former monopoly provider will respond by increasing the size of its network because having the larger network is its economic advantage.'

Railway managers had been telling parliament every year that increased competition would force them to close branch lines and concentrate on the main trunk line. 'It isn't so,' said Chuck. 'Competition will force the organisation to widen its network.'

New Zealand Rail – a Wellington suburban train. (*Evening Post Collection, Alexander Turnbull Library, Wellington, NZ, F-32140-1/4*)

IMPLEMENTING CHANGE

Commentators had failed to notice that the rail network, which had been shrinking year by year, stopped reducing once New Zealand Rail had to compete. No rail line closed while I was minister. Indeed, in a way, the rail network has increased; railways now has the biggest truck fleet in the country. This piece of knowledge was to have a profound effect on my policy. When Air New Zealand told me that if I allowed Ansett Airlines to compete it would have to cancel provincial services, I was able to accurately predict that provincial services would increase. Air New Zealand may lose money flying passengers from Invercargill to Dunedin, but those same passengers may fly on to London and because they started on Air New Zealand, they are more likely to stay on the airline. Prior to competition many provincial services had just one Air New Zealand flight a day, now they have many air services.

New Zealand Railways

Logo of the former New Zealand Rail Ltd.
(*Courtesy of ONTRACK and Toll NZ*)

New Zealand Post also told me that rural services would suffer through competition. As Hoppe's law states, not so. Rural services have never been better. The rural network is the competitive advantage. Customers such as Inland Revenue want to be able to write to everyone, so they must use New Zealand Post's service. The rural telephone network is also Telecom's competitive advantage. No rural service has been cut.

Chuck then asked me why I was in America. I explained that I had a ten-day, all-expenses-paid visit and that I wanted to see the latest in transport. Not just railways but also ports. I said I would like to see American Airlines to find out why they were not visiting New Zealand. It had been suggested to me that I should see the Port of New York. Chuck had a long reach, and he fixed it all for me.

The trip was everything he promised. I saw computerised ports where containers were loaded from the ship straight on to the decks of slow-moving trains. No double handling. I found out an important fact explaining why American Airlines had stopped serving New Zealand. It was because the curfew at Sydney meant the 747 arrived in LA so late that it caused timetable problems across the American Airlines network. The tail was wagging the dog so we had been removed from the schedule. (As minister I resisted calls for curfews and believed local bodies should refuse to allow residential building in the flight paths.)

I also watched US railroads achieve productivity levels not dreamed of in New Zealand. I remember describing the shunting yard at Franklin where trains are made up. New Zealand Rail was very proud of it. The US railroad man said:

IMPLEMENTING CHANGE

'We try not to shunt trains at all, it damages freight.' But how do they run a railroad without shunting? 'We load the trains in the order that we want in the first place,' the US railroad man said. It sounds obvious but it had not occurred to New Zealand Rail. Actually, it hadn't occurred to me either.

When I later said these things were possible, people in the New Zealand transport industry said they were not. But I believed they were because I'd seen them work with my own eyes.

When I joined the Mainfreight board I found that company had also sent people to America to learn the latest techniques. I strongly recommend this practice to any industry that wants to achieve. Go and see for yourself. Americans are wonderfully open and to them I guess they are helping a third-world nation.

No railway manager had ever visited a US railroad, even though US railroads are the world leaders. This anti-American bias existed throughout the civil service. Even today advice is being sought from Britain. Considering the British track record on rail, this isn't exactly achievement thinking.

So, in the event, I was not surprised that Chuck had fascinated the conference as much as he'd fascinated me the year before.

Michael, as our facilitator, suggested we break into small groups to discuss the report, and then to report back our findings.

He gave us an introductory exercise. It was shorter than the desert-survival exercise but was also designed to get groups to work together. We had to read an account of an armed robbery and then answer some questions. First individually, and then the group had to agree on the answers.

In order to involve MPs in the process, I had got a group of Labour backbenchers to act as facilitators. I recall what happened in the Lindsay Paps group. He was horrified to find himself in a group with a long-haired worker who had tattoos down his arms. He was a shunter. Worse than a member of the public. Every instinct in the chairman's body led him to shut the shunter out of the discussion and ignore his ideas. In the chairman's manner he got the group to adopt his answers. Loyalty, obedience, respect were still the cardinal virtues on the railroad. It was comical to observe his face as he discovered how poor his group's score was. He was even more shocked to discover that the shunter's answers were far more accurate than his own. To his credit, for the rest of the summit Lindsay Pap listened very closely and very carefully to every word that tattooed, long-haired shunter said.

> As we found with the nation, once employees accept that real change is needed, people prefer radical change so they know where they are.

What the exercise showed was that groups usually outperform individuals. And that simple insight got people listening to one another – in their own interest.

The results of the conference exceeded all my expectations. I had hoped just to get an acceptance that real change was needed and then to begin the long, hard negotiation and horse-trading to get where we had to go. They'd all got there already. The groups came back unanimous. One-man trains, fewer and longer trains, fewer workshops and a redundancy scheme to shed staff quickly. In all the controversy that followed in the media and in the community, it was forgotten that what we did was to implement an industry plan agreed by management and workers alike – but particularly by the workers.

Why? How? I'll tell you what it was. The railwaymen loved trains. They would go and ride rail systems on their holidays. Their knowledge of their part of the system always exceeded that of management.

As we found with the nation, once employees accept that real change is needed, people prefer radical change so they know where they are.

Achieving change

THE BREAKTHROUGH AT the conference came from an exercise called force field analysis. The exercise requires you to identify not just the forces for change – in railways' case, competition from road transport – but also the restraining forces, those preventing change.

What was it – actually – that was preventing rail from adapting to meet the road competition? The rail employees identified half of the restraining force very quickly. It was the fear of being made compulsorily redundant. If that fear were removed, then radical change was possible.

The conference revealed the workers were more in favour of radical change than management was, provided the change was fair.

This was an experience that was to be repeated time and again. In every government business I found that the people most reluctant to advocate change were those in management. They would say, 'Yes this change is desirable but the unions will never accept it. It cannot be done.'

So time and again, I went directly to the workforce. In every case the workers were well aware of the need for

OUT OF THE RED

Wanganui workshops, 1986. Looks closed, but actually it was 'working'. (*Wanganui Chronicle*)

Visiting the Wanganui workshops in 1984. (*Wanganui Chronicle*)

ACHIEVING CHANGE

I first met Ross when I was a student writing a dissertation on import licensing for my law degree. (It is one of life's ironies that, as the writer of the textbook on import licensing, I voted for its abolition.) Ross made an immediate difference to the railways. From the little things to the big . . .

He mentioned to me one day that he had been walking through the administration office of the Auckland railway station and he noticed that the workers were dialling up their calls from memory. He asked, 'How are you able to telephone without looking up the number?' The answer was that they were calling New Zealand Rail's big customers about their accounts and there were just thirty major customers so they knew the numbers. 'How often do you ring?' 'Some, many times a day, all of them at least once a week.'

The workers were using old dial phones. 'So I have ordered them automatic dialling phones. The stationmaster is horrified. Only senior management are allowed memory telephones. I have pointed out that these workers, by collecting from our biggest customers, are our biggest earners. They will be able to make more calls and just one call could pay for the whole system.'

I had been through the same office and had failed to notice this. I also visited the workshops on many occasions. I had noticed that there were piles of rusty iron sheets. Ross, as an accountant, when he went through realised that the metal was valuable. It was rusty, which meant the iron had been there a while. He did an immediate check and realised that the railway workshops inventory was excessive. He sold the excess stock and saved the railways millions.

I found Ross' advice to be excellent. We met each week

Ross Sayers. (*New Zealand Herald/APN*)

I recruited Ross when I read in the *New Zealand Herald* that he was leaving Lion Breweries. He had already received two offers for double the money that I could offer but I had an irresistible challenge – the railways.

and occasionally lied to their members about management's proposals.

It still amazes me that some union officials think they have the right to tell any lie. I also find it extraordinary that the present government's industrial law makes it illegal to communicate any wage offer directly to your employees. This is a scandal. It is a contravention of human rights. The only thing that isn't surprising is that it's government policy.

I am sure that redundancy was accepted because we wrote directly to the guards' homes. What happened was that the wife opened the letter; she read the offer, which was a good one, and then said to her husband, 'Accept the redundancy, we can pay off the mortgage and you can take that job that my brother has been offering you.'

Both management and union were convinced that rail employees would not take the redundancy package. In time, the number of railway employees went from twenty-two thousand to seven thousand with fewer than twenty employees being made compulsorily redundant. The unions refused to support the handful of workers who refused to retrain, would not relocate and just demanded to be employed in a job that did not exist. The media continued to report mass rail redundancies without telling their readers that they were voluntary.

Many people played a part in rail's turnaround. Most were railway employees like Dr Francis Small who was a manager when the organisation was losing a million a day and general manager when it came into profit. The man who played a key role in introducing the private-sector culture and taught me a great deal about successful management was Ross Sayers.

I brought a stop to the talk of a strike when I asked a quiet question: 'Who is going to tell the guards who have applied for redundancy that they cannot have it?'

I recall one particularly militant union member from Napier who said, 'No one is going to apply, I sent back my application saying I would only accept redundancy if New Zealand Rail also paid for my relocation to Australia.'

'I know that you have applied for redundancy,' I replied. 'In your case, I have authorised your airfare, even though I am sure it is at the expense of good trans-Tasman relationships.' He then tried to say it was just a joke but he had destroyed his credibility. (I did urge New Zealand Rail to accept his offer but they felt they could not. He went on to cause trouble for three years before quietly accepting a redundancy package.)

The general secretary, who was more cautious, then asked how many people had applied. 'We want forty and since Monday we have received over 120,' I said. I could see the general secretary imagining facing 120 angry railway workers and 120 of their angry wives (and maybe a few mistresses). The strike threat was over.

> A sensible firm always keeps contact with its employees' families.

A sensible firm always keeps contact with its employees' families. I found that there were many state businesses that did not know their employees' addresses. They communicated with their employees via the union. The unions often distorted radical change and often urged me to go further and faster.

We did the maths and it showed that even a redundancy package that could give an employee more than a year's wages in a lump sum was the best investment New Zealand Rail could make. The Treasury likes a 10 per cent return on investment in a year. If you look at it in a certain way, these redundancy packages of a year's salary were paying a 100 per cent rate of return. In less than a year, rail was saving money.

Redundancy payment was very attractive because the IRD regarded it as largely a capital payment and taxed it at 5 per cent. I still think that is right. We were buying the knowledge and experience employees had in their jobs, a capital investment. Bill Birch introduced a law change to tax all redundancy payments as income. National and Labour's hostility to 'golden goodbyes' misunderstands that redundancy is a win–win deal. The employee is compensated for the loss of employment; the organisation wins by being able to implement needed reform. The state should be encouraging, not opposing, such flexibility.

When we announced we were phasing out guards on trains and introducing a voluntary redundancy scheme, I insisted that the details of the generous package be sent to every guard at home.

The NUR threatened to call a nationwide stoppage. We held an emergency talk in my office. The NUR thought that the guards, not having had a real job, would be unemployable. They could not argue that guards were needed on trains. Even though they knew a strike would be financially disastrous for rail, the union felt it had to act for its members.

to talk about the railways but I also took the chance to raise issues with him that I had in my other portfolios. He gave me two pieces of advice that I found to be sound.

The first was to watch the cash. 'A clever accountant can, for a period, get the books to say almost anything. What he can't do is create cash. No cash is always a bad sign.'

> Advice number one: watch the cash.

I have only done a short course in accounting but I all I had to do was apply the Sayers Principle and watch the cash. The accounts presented by many government departments just defy interpretation. So when I saw the cash was dwindling, I would say, 'I think there is trouble at this particular mill. Let's review the operation.' It always turned out that there was a problem. Sometimes even the management was not aware of the rapidly deteriorating situation. So advice number one: watch the cash.

Railways not having any intelligible accounts appalled Ross. Effective leaders always want to know all the facts. When he found out the facts he understood why they'd been kept secret so long. Like the mad old relation kept chained in the attic, the facts were appalling.

If every private engineering workshop in the country closed, railways' four civil engineering shops would still have excess capacity.

The Wanganui workshop, being remote and on a branch line, was the obvious candidate for closure. I was reluctant because Wanganui was a railway town. I thought that closing a workshop employing over 350 people would have a massive effect on a small town.

I recall visiting the works and being proudly shown a computer-controlled lathe that could shape metal within thousands of a centimetre, work day and night, seven days a week, requiring only one semi-skilled operator. 'The machine does work that used to require fourteen skilled workers. They could never achieve this accuracy.'

'What happened to the men?' I asked. The answer was they were still employed but only to watch the machine do the jobs they once did.

During the election campaign I had refused to give an undertaking to keep the works open. The Wanganui paper had attacked me on its front page for my refusal. This did not stop the paper from later attacking me for the closure.

The local MP Russell Marshall had, even after I had privately told him that the workshops would close, promised that the government would keep them open. He even said he would resign over it.

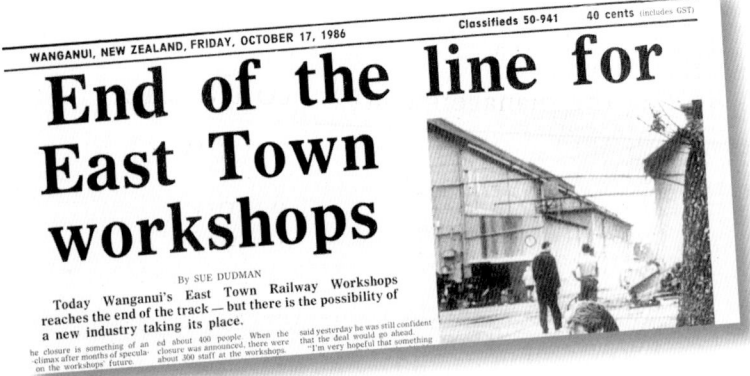

ACHIEVING CHANGE

It was a hard decision. Officials brought in Russell's press release and asked if we should now close a different workshop. 'No,' I said. 'If it gets out I buckled to blackmail, half of parliament will be threatening to resign.'

There is a saying in politics that the art is to announce all good news yourself and have your underlings announce all bad news. Prime ministers like to announce good news and get junior ministers or even better, officials, to announce the bad. (Helen Clark is the master of this dark art.)

Railways was so demoralised and its problems so great that I told management, 'I will announce the bad news. When you get good news it will be the result of your work and you can announce it.'

I called a press conference and announced the closure of the Wanganui workshops. I took the heat from Russell Marshall, the mayor, the media, the unions and the workers.

Such a policy did not make me popular but had the merit of making the managers courageous. It turned into one of those principles that guided me. If you want the respect of your employees, make it clear that you are prepared to do the toughest jobs. Announcing bad news is one of the toughest.

> If you want the respect of your employees, make it clear that you are prepared to do the toughest jobs. Announcing bad news is one of the toughest.

> If you will not admit you have made a mistake but instead blame others, you will create an organisation that is in denial.

I also tried to encourage a culture of facing problems by admitting my own failures. I did not always win Cabinet endorsement. I would tell my managers immediately of my failure. I sought to create a culture where mistakes are quickly acknowledged so they can be addressed. If you will not admit you have made a mistake but instead blame others, you will create an organisation that is in denial. If you're in denial you are more likely to collaborate in other people's denial as a quid pro quo. It's easy to see how cultures can turn rotten.

The furore over the Wanganui closure died down. Six months later, fewer than a dozen employees were out of work. Employment in the town increased. The railways realised that they were no longer an employment scheme but a transport company willing to do what it took to become efficient. More efficient businesses created more jobs.

Minister of almost everything

BEING MADE THE minister of twenty-one different businesses overnight is a bit of a challenge. First things first, I thought. Let's meet the chief executives of all twenty-one. I had my staff schedule a forty-minute meeting with each of the general managers. Time was tight. I recall that one manager wasn't having any of it. He protested he worked for his board, not for the minister. I was happy to meet his successor the following week, appointed by a new board if necessary. He turned up.

Mr Prebble Big Winner In Cabinet Stakes

The headline sounds good, but the reality was somewhat different!

How do you get twenty-one different businesses to report when you know little about the organisations? I just asked each manager for his results for the last twelve months, and what would be the results for the next quarter and coming year? I listened as each manager told me why he was making a loss and had not reached his forecast. They all said they needed more capital. I asked how much and when. I totalled all the requests; it was more than the New Zealand Government's annual budget. They then told me that with the capital injection they could make a profit, without it they estimated the loss they would make. Railways' loss was over 350 million dollars. Call it a billion in today's money. It was a shunting shed full of money.

I then used Ross Sayers' second piece of advice and asked as cunning a question as the civil service had ever heard: 'How is the computer program? Is it as bad as I hear?' Out it all came, with all the relief of a confession too long withheld. It was always the same; a revelation of huge expenditure on a world-leading, world-beating, world-class computer system. The one thing all these systems had in common was that they didn't work.

My favourite is the computer that spoke Swedish. Keeping track of telephone lines is a nightmare. New Zealand Post realised that a phone company overseas must have a computer program to do this and found that Swedish Telecom had an excellent one. The general manager explained the Swedes sold it for just two million dollars. New Zealand Post had allowed another two million dollars to get it to speak English but eighteen months and thirty-seven million dollars later it still did not work.

'Why don't you just pull the plug?' I said. 'But we have spent so much.' 'Will it ever speak English?' I asked. And the answer was, 'Not properly'.

I formed the view that the best we could hope for was a sort of Danish. When officials are publicly blamed, even for ministers' mistakes, there is a culture of never reporting bad news or admitting mistakes.

In 2005, schoolteachers knew by August that the scholarship exam was flawed. No one told the prime minister until February, after the exam results had been posted.

I think the officials would still be in denial that buying a computer program that did not speak English was a mistake. I wrote a note there and then, authorising the cancellation of the program and told the manager not to waste another dollar. Business knows not to spend money on a mistake, but what if you are not allowed to admit to having made a mistake?

I asked the general manager of New Zealand Post if it was true he was looking at closing post offices. The previous postmaster general, the Rt Hon Jonathan Hunt, had repeatedly told parliament that he knew of no plans to close any post office. His statement was correct but untrue. The only reason he could make the statement was because he refused to allow New Zealand Post to brief him on the subject. Why did he refuse? Because he knew what it would tell him.

'I thought you might ask me that,' said the general manager.

'I have brought the list with me'. I skimmed through the pages of proposed closures. 'How many are there?' I asked. The answer was 432. 'Are all of these post offices surplus?' 'Yes.' The remaining network could easily provide the service. If the surplus branches stayed open we would need a multi-million dollar subsidy. 'Is this first page of branch closures typical?' I asked. Indeed they were, the general manager assured me sadly. 'How is it that half of the post offices on the first page are in my electorate?' I asked.

'Are they, minister?'

Are they, minister? Are they? That list I remember as a perfect example of what is known in politics as the Washington Monument. They say that whenever the civil service in America is asked to make expenditure cuts, they recommend closing the Washington Monument. They know no politician would ever do so.

Here was my moment to order the closure of the Washington Monument. I took the list and wrote on it 'Approved', signed it and gave it back to the general manager.

It is a huge waste of time having managers asking for twice what they want while hoping they will get half. After the post office branch closures, I never had any of the SOEs testing me out.

As it happened, I had a delegation from the Irish postal services which I was forced to keep waiting. I explained to the delegation that I had just agreed to close 432 post offices. I also said that I had agreed as minister to make the statement announcing the closures myself, as part of my policy of announcing all bad news. 'They are all going to close on the same day,' I explained. 'The earliest date they can close is

February; it can't be February the sixth, which is our national day, and the seventh is my birthday, so they will have to close on the eighth.'

Closing 432 post offices on one day is not sensible or businesslike. I would have much preferred to have a programme of orderly closures of surplus branches together with the opening of new services. Jonathan Hunt's well-known refusal to agree to any post office branch closing, no matter how redundant it was, had made the issue of closures a test of government's resolve. The irony is that New Zealand Post opened new services in more than a thousand shops.

(*New Zealand Listener*)

The network, which had been frozen, almost doubled and a whole range of new services was introduced. The media are not interested in good news so it became a myth that I had reduced the post office network.

The Irish post officials told me the Irish postal services had been corporatised some years earlier and since then they had been able to close twelve branches in remote villages where the postmistress had died and no one was willing to take the job. They were amazed at my decision. Even more amazed that I myself was going to announce the closures.

The reforms certainly worked. New Zealand Post had lost millions of dollars each year and was so slow in delivering letters, it was likely to be true when people said, 'The cheque is in the mail'. New Zealand Post not only became profitable, it introduced a next-day delivery service and the cost of posting a standard letter was reduced from forty-five cents to forty.

A few years later I was invited to give a speech on New Zealand's postal reforms to the international postal union, a meeting of the world's postal services. It wasn't a naturally sympathetic audience. They took particular exception to the news that we had removed the postal monopoly. I told them bluntly that government had no role in what was really a message service. Our national postal service should be privatised and the international postal union should review its rules that assumed the world's post offices were government monopolies.

The Dutch manager said that our reforms would only work in a small country like New Zealand and not in the Netherlands with its remote rural areas. There are people overseas who like saying things like this about New Zealand. I pointed out the Netherlands would fit into New Zealand many times over and the South Island was a land mass with mountains higher than the Alps.

The French manager told the conference that I was a liar. The performance figures I had given, he knew from a lifetime in the French postal service, could not be achieved. They were *inscrutable*! *Vive la France!* It was a conference hall full of enraged postal managers. They were so angry I thought I was going to be booed off the stage.

The American postal regulator – of the world's largest post office – was sharing the panel. He saved me. He told the audience that he had only accepted the invitation to speak in order to hear me. He then produced a whole range of technical statistics about New Zealand Post's performance. Some were news to me. He told the astonished audience, 'Mr Prebble is the greatest postal reformer of the twentieth century.' *Sacre bleu!* I only repeat the story because I like it and because our media never will.

Problem-solving

RULE NUMBER ONE: when problem-solving, gather all the information. Rule number two: separate the collection of information from the judgement stage.

Rule one is harder than it looks and rule two is much harder still. But it is very, very important, because as soon as you start judging, you will dismiss unhelpful facts as irrelevant.

In order to separate the information-gathering stage from the judgement stage, I kept a whiteboard in the office. In any important discussion, I'd say, 'Let's just put down all the facts about the issue'. Only when we had reached an agreement that all available facts were up there could we agree what the problem was. Only then could we start generating solutions.

New Zealand Post had a problem. It had found that rural deliveries had been costing it money. It had leased out routes to private contractors. We whiteboarded the problem. The postal service was losing money yet contractors were willing to pay for the right to deliver the mail. It did not make sense.

Legally, the routes belonged to New Zealand Post. The contractors' services varied greatly. New Zealand Post wanted to get back control by putting all the routes up for tender. This was very unpopular with people who had inherited their routes or had bought them.

Be that as it may, I thought New Zealand Post was right; the goodwill belonged to the taxpayer. The organisation not only had the right to manage its network, it had a duty to do so. Nonetheless, I felt sympathy for the rural contractors. Taking both points of view on board, I said that if the existing contactor were outbid he must be given the opportunity to match the winning bid.

To the surprise of New Zealand Post, contractors bid far more than expected. In the few cases when they were outbid, nearly all the existing contractors decided to match the winning bid. Rural delivery contractors also delivered bread, milk and parcels for their customers. This business was far more profitable than New Zealand Post had realised.

Two rural mail contractors in the remote King Country refused to match winning bids and set up their own mail service in competition. It was illegal to deliver mail in competition with New Zealand Post. Management asked me to declare the services illegal. I declined to act, pointing out that the postal service had always claimed rural mail lost money.

'If you are right and rural mail is unprofitable, they will go out of business.'

The contractors not only prospered but also soon announced they were lowering the price of their stamps to thirty-five cents. Those contractors are the reason we

PROBLEM-SOLVING

removed the postal monopoly. Now anyone can deliver mail in New Zealand and there are many services. The lawyers have their own mail service for legal documents.

To get an organisation to change, there has to be a reason, some threat. I do not believe that I am a great postal reformer and I had little to do with the reforms. It was competition that was the great reformer of New Zealand's postal service.

> To get an organisation to change, there has to be a reason, some threat.

Putting out fires

FROM DAY ONE I faced an issue that has defeated successive governments: reforming the crash fire service. Everyone has a view on the fire service. The nation has even held a referendum on how many firemen should man a fire engine. The only thing everyone was in agreement on was that the problems in the airport crash fire service were appalling.

The crash of an Air New Zealand Friendship into the Manakau Harbour leads to an inquiry into the crash fire services.
(*New Zealand Herald/APN*)

A number of high-profile incidents, like the one illustrated by the front-page photograph of a crashed aeroplane at Auckland airport stuck in the mudflats, had led the previous government to set up the Beecham report.

In those pre-Freedom of Information Act days, the report was secret. The state union, the Public Service Association (PSA), was campaigning against the report and again I promised to publish it.

At my first meeting with officials on becoming minister of civil aviation, I said we would be publishing the report into crash fire services. 'Yes, of course minister, but will you be publishing it before you've read the Smith report?'

'What is the Smith report?' I asked.

'It is the report we commissioned into the Beecham report.'

'I will have to read it.' I said, 'But we must publish it too.'

'Yes, of course minister, but will you be publishing it before you've read the Shepherd report?'

I asked: 'Just how many reports have you done into the crash fire service?'

'In the last nine years?' they said. 'Four.'

'How many of the reports' recommendations have you implemented?'

'None,' they said.

Not one. Four reports. How many man-hours, or man-years had gone into writing these reports that were not only never implemented but never meant to be implemented?

It was then I decided to request all the reports the ministry of transport had commissioned in the past decade.

'Are you sure minister?' said the secretary of transport (always a warning sign). I asked why he was questioning my request. 'The reports will make a stack two metres high. You won't have time to read them.' I said I still wanted the reports. The man was right. I did not have time to read them but I did measure them: over two metres of reading. Two hundred centimetres. I asked him how much had been implemented. A hundred centimetres? Fifty? 'Less than ten,' was his reply.

I did read the reports into the crash fire service. I learnt that in World War II many planes caught fire and the pilots suffered terrible burns. As a result every airport had a crash fire service.

Roger Smith, a Wellington accountant who had authored the follow-up report, had done an analysis of air accidents in New Zealand since World War II. He found that the New Zealand crash fire service had never saved a passenger. He then statistically analysed world aviation for the last two years and found that no passenger anywhere in the world had been saved by an airport crash fire service. He also managed to calculate, somehow, that the chances of the crash fire service ever saving a passenger were nil. This is because planes, when they crash, tend to miss the airport so the crash fire engines cannot reach the plane on time. He recommended that the crash fire service at airports be disbanded.

I had problems with this recommendation. I did not think the public would accept Mr Smith's statistically impressive calculations. Even those of us who knew the odds took comfort from the sight of the crash fire trucks on the runway. More importantly, under multilateral aviation agreements

PUTTING OUT FIRES

New Zealand is bound to provide crash fire services at all international airports. It's part of international air law.

I asked one of my staff to give the good accountant a ring and ask him how he expected the minister to implement his recommendations. Mr Smith advised us he did not expect the findings to be implemented at all. He was reporting the ideal.

I resolved not to call for another report of any sort while I was minister for transport. The most common reports are inquiries. The whole transport sector was paralysed with fear at the thought of an inquiry. Most accidents are a result of a combination of carelessness, misjudgement and bad luck. It is very rare that an accident is the result of an inadequacy in the safety regulations. After having spent three months and hundreds of thousands of dollars on the inquiry, the commissioners feel they cannot say that it was just an accident. They feel obliged to recommend new expensive safety standards. Even though, if the existing standards had been followed, the accident would not have happened. The minister comes under huge pressure to implement the commission of inquiry's expensive recommendations. A significant proportion of red tape in the transport sector is the result of recommendations from commissions of inquiry.

I think I'm the only minister of transport who would have refused, as I did, to order an inquiry into the sinking of the *Mikhail Lermontov*, the Russian passenger ship. It is the biggest civilian sinking in the world since World War II. We all knew the reason for the sinking. The New Zealand pilot steered the boat onto rocks. He knew the rocks were there. He will never be able to explain what happened. There was nothing wrong with our marine regulations. No more passenger liners have sunk. If I had set up an inquiry, some judge would have felt obliged to make a series of expensive recommendations.

The crash fire service was costing tens of millions of dollars a year. The reports indicated that the service was excessive but gave no guidance about what to do. The crash firemen themselves, having nothing to do, were extremely militant. Ministers had been paralysed by threats from the union that if there were any changes, they would go on strike. The pilots said that if the crash fire service was on strike then they would not fly. What to do?

I asked Michael what Human Synergistics would recommend. He asked me the obvious question. 'Has anyone ever consulted with the crash firemen as to what they believe should happen?' I thought that was a good question. I asked the director of civil aviation who was shocked. 'They are militant unionists who will just make more demands.'

I said, 'We've tried everything else. Let's ask the men themselves.' The director asked me how I thought the consultation should be conducted and I said I got the idea from Human Synergistics.

Michael and his team flew to each airport and called the crash firemen together and asked them how they thought the minister should respond to the issues that had been raised. It was just like a mini-railway summit. Just as in the railway summit, they did the card sort. That's when you write down your own ideas on a card and put it back into the stack. The cards are shuffled and given out so you don't speak to your own idea. The team then groups the ideas into topics and evaluates them. It's a wonderful way of separating personalities from the issues.

Human Synergistics returned with a set of proposals that had the consensus support of the nation's crash firemen. And guess what? The proposals were sane, sensible and practical – and they exceeded anything put forward by management. (Management was pretty toey about it, when it saw what the militant union had come up with.) The crash firemen proposed a scaling back of services and that they take on extra responsibilities such as security. They also asked to be consulted on equipment.

It turned out the department had had the practice of purchasing very expensive kits without asking the firefighters. The resulting problems: equipment waiting for parts and fire trucks too heavy to be used on the grass surrounds of airports.

The crash firemen, who had plenty of time to think about what equipment they really needed, had some very practical suggestions. Over the department's objections, I accepted the report in total. Not only has the report saved tens of millions of dollars but also there has been no trade union militancy in the crash fire service. Despite our

> **Employees prefer to work for an efficient organisation and employees usually know not only what is wrong but also often how to fix it.**

success, it has not occurred to subsequent governments to ask the nation's firefighters for their ideas on how the fire service should be run.

It is my universal experience that employees prefer to work for an efficient organisation and employees usually know not only what is wrong but also often how to fix it. The trick is how to ask for their help.

Group decision-making

I WAS SYMPATHETIC to the position of a government backbencher. The Lange Labour Government was introducing radical reforms; floating the dollar, introducing a goods and services tax, abolishing subsidies, deregulating the financial sector and, my area, corporatising and now proposing privatisation. The MPs who faced tough election challenges were getting nervous.

After a number of difficult caucus meetings it was decided to have a three-day caucus in the rural town of Ashburton. Those MPs who remembered our retreat at Tatum Park asked if Michael Gourley could facilitate the caucus.

It was one of the more memorable caucuses. Michael used a process called group role negotiation to allow the backbenchers to express their frustrations with ministers and for the Cabinet to express its annoyance with caucus. One of the problems was that caucus meetings, which were held every Thursday, lasted just two and a half hours. There were over sixty MPs. That meant each MP had less than three minutes to speak. Not long enough to discuss topics like fundamental tax reform.

The original Lange Cabinet. (*Michael Bassett*)

The caucus worked out what came to be called the Ashburton Accord. The Cabinet agreed to consult with caucus early and to reduce surprises as far as possible. The caucus, for its part, agreed to work consultatively and not though the media.

I recall one issue was that ministers tended to work with their particular caucus committee. MPs who were not on the finance committee but were interested in the economy, felt out of the loop. We finance ministers agreed to hold a session in the caucus room every Wednesday night open to any MP. For some weeks every Wednesday night I led a discussion with MPs on SOEs.

I used the Human Synergistics approach. For the first few sessions I insisted that we simply examine in depth why we had government businesses. I refused to move on to topics like how many post offices we had, and how many we should have, and where they should be, until we were all in agreement on why there were government-owned post offices at all. Why did government own businesses? Why these businesses and not others? How did it start?

I did some research to try to find the answers. There were many reasons and many of them weren't good. What I was taught at school – that the British Government invented the penny post – is wrong. A Scot invented it and the British Government tried to buy it from him. When he refused to sell, an Act of Parliament was passed taking it from him. But why did the state want a post office? Oliver Cromwell told parliament that 'mischievous messages' were being sent and proposed that the delivery of messages be a state monopoly so the government could read the mail. That may have made sense in a time of civil war but here we were, nearly four hundred years later, with the government hardly able to deliver the mischievous messages, let alone read them all.

The government got into coal mining in World War II as a temporary measure. The government wanted production of coal increased to what was an uneconomic level in order to defeat the Nazis. The government could not agree with the mine owners how much to buy the coal for, so they bought the mines instead. It was a solution, of sorts. The Nazis were long gone by the time of my whiteboard, but we still owned the mines.

There's a story of a westerner visiting Russia in the nineteenth century. He noticed that a soldier came to stand at a particular point in the empty square in front of his hotel for an hour every day, from three to four o'clock. It turned out he was on guard duty for the Tsar's children who were playing in the garden behind the wall. Except the garden had gone, the wall had been knocked down and the children had grown up. But no one had told the military and standing orders had it that the guard should perform guard duty at that spot and at that time. We scoff at the absurdity of it – but we did still own coal mines on the same principles of inertia and conservatism.

I brought out the whiteboard and asked what we wanted out of government businesses. What did we want? Quality service for the public? Put it up. Jobs for workers? Put it up. Natural monopolies? Up it went. Solving market failures? That too. A reasonable rate of return on taxpayers' investment? Got to have that. A dividend, now that SOEs were getting their act together? Certainly. What else was there? We couldn't think of anything else. No one quite dared say: to control the means of production and distribution in order to create a dictatorship of the proletariat. But if it had been offered I would have put it up on the board (where it would have looked very out of place – such is the power of the whiteboard).

MPs were shocked to learn that in the 150 years the New Zealand Government had owned businesses, there had never been a year where the businesses had not cost the taxpayer money. Even the government's most successful business, State Insurance, had never paid a dividend.

The State Owned Enterprise Act has a provision for parliament to pay a state business to provide a service where there is market failure. In twenty years only one subsidy has ever been paid for – the provision of rural banking services – now done by ATM machines. Market failure is a myth.

MPs realised that these businesses were a huge risk. Even a very profitable enterprise like Telecom is risky. Which new technology will be a winner? Officials told me that teletext was the future and that fax machines would never take off. They still had a warehouse full of dial-up telephone sets (they might come back). The government's record at assessing risk was poor. Private enterprise makes similar mistakes, but the companies that make them are swiftly and brutally punished, often with extinction. Governments go on and on making the same mistakes again and again (practice makes perfect, after all).

As a result of years of deficit spending and the failure of the Muldoon Government's massive Think Big engineering schemes, New Zealand was heavily in debt. It made more sense to us – and even to Helen Clark and Michael Cullen – to sell risky state businesses and repay debt. We came to realise that even if we did not face a debt crisis, privatisation is a sensible policy.

> If you can separate the emotion and the personalities and examine what the real problem really is . . . the solution may be something you never considered.

(*Courtesy of Garrick Tremain*)

These Wednesday-night discussions were the reason that Labour MPs voted to privatise large areas of the state sector. If you can separate the emotion and the personalities and examine what the real problem really is . . . the solution may be something you never considered. Privatisation was a policy none of us had expected. But very few of us resisted the logic.

Out of the red

PEOPLE OFTEN ASK how it is that I, who was a Labour MP, could have been part of a government that introduced more free enterprise than any government before or since. How is it that now I am part of the ACT Party that advocates individual choice, low flat tax and less government? I give a number of answers to explain my journey across the political landscape. In the case of privatisation, having been in charge of the government's businesses I know from experience that governments are not good at making commercial decisions.

In some important ways my views have not changed from those I held as a seventeen-year-old when I joined the Labour Party.

I have always believed in a society where everyone has an opportunity to participate. My family was very poor. My two older brothers qualified for free boarding-school education from the remarkable Dilworth Trust that pays for the education of poor children. I too was to go to Dilworth, but the Anglican Church was shamed into paying its clergy a living wage.

I am grateful that New Zealand made it possible for my

> What I have always opposed is privilege.

four brothers, my sister, and me to have a university education. I want others to have the same opportunity to succeed. Equal opportunity is not the same as equality. Some will take their chances and others will not. Society will never be equal; some have more talent than others. What I have always opposed is privilege.

It seemed to me in my youth that the Labour Party was the party of equal opportunity and National of privilege. Today I am not so sure. Labour is granting privileges to trade unions that discriminate against non-unionists. I feel today's Labour Party sees the country as many groups competing for resources. Women, Maori, workers, Pacific Islanders and ethnic groups competing with one another and against Labour's new class enemy, the white middle-aged male, a tribe I have some affection for.

> A government that is powerful enough to take from others and give it to you is powerful enough to take all that you have away.

Labour sees its role as being to take from some groups and give to others. The socialist goal of equality can only be achieved when we all have nothing. It is not a legitimate role

My journey across the political landscape.
Above: Me in the 1980s.
Below: Me, August 2005. (*New Zealand Herald/APN*)

for government to take from its citizens to give to others. A government that is powerful enough to take from others and give it to you is powerful enough to take all that you have away.

I was never a socialist but I did think that government should own key industries for all the arguments we rehearsed on the Wednesday-night whiteboards. I thought that government would do a better job. The New Zealand civil service is honest and professional. Most civil servants put in a fair day's work and the senor civil servants work very hard. So I was shocked when I found how wasteful the state businesses are.

At first I blamed previous governments. If the state trading enterprises had a strong able minister (for example, me) I was sure good results would follow.

When I became the minister, Air New Zealand's domestic service can only be described as soviet. The airline's internal monopoly did not know the meaning of service.

Planes departed so far behind schedule that I got in the habit of leaving the city for the airport in Wellington at the time the flight was supposed to be leaving. I rarely missed a flight. The airline refused to build air bridges and in a country where it rains every other day, passengers were often soaked. The pilots, stewards and engineers took turns to strike in the holidays.

As the new minister I learnt that just 10 per cent of flights took off on time. 'All this is going to change.' I thought. 'Like Mussolini, I will get the planes to fly on time.' I fired the board and appointed top businessmen, gave the airline the new planes it wanted, delivered the unions a pep talk and after one year just 10 per cent of planes flew on time.

When I gave Ansett Airlines permission to fly in competition, suddenly – practically overnight – the planes were flying on time. Air New Zealand also provided air bridges and lounges, food for passengers and reduced airfares. Flights to provincial centres jumped from one a day to several. Free enterprise competition achieved in weeks everything that the government had failed to achieve in years of trying.

I had to rethink my views.

I realised why governments cannot run businesses. The politicians are trying to win elections. A tried and proved formula is to bribe the voters. We don't use illegal methods but cat-skinning comes in many different forms. When I became minister in charge of Telecom there were a hundred thousand free phones. Politicians had granted free phones to a whole range of worthy organisations, all to win votes. I say 'free' but there's no such thing as a free phone. Other customers and the taxpayer paid.

> **Free enterprise competition achieved in weeks everything that the government had failed to achieve in years of trying.**

Who should have a free phone was more important to politicians than fixing the telephone system. With waiting lists for new connections of up to three years, you needed an MP to get you hooked up. I became an expert at getting phones for constituents and it did me no harm at the ballot box. I was on very good terms with a certain clerk buried deep in New Zealand Post – he was the fellow who decided whether you were going to get a phone or not (he should have been on the One Hundred Most Powerful Men in New Zealand List for 1977 – and in the top half of the list).

This part of old New Zealand had a lot of charm, in its way. You'd book a call to talk to your friend on the East Coast and the local operator might say, 'The Mackenzies are having a party tonight, I'll put your call through to the bach.' Of course, she'd probably listen to your call as well (it was worse in Fiji at the time when they'd put interesting phone calls on the loudspeaker system).

The airline had a similarly personal level of service. I remember 'Taxi' Frank Rogers pulling off one of the more successful operations of his career when he got me to hold his tormentor Aussie Malcolm in conversation in the departure lounge. Frank got ahead and into his seat. A few minutes later the whole plane (MPs, lobbyists, the front row of the political class) witnessed Aussie: 'Frank look at you, you can't do anything right. You're in my seat. Up you get, Frank! Up you get! Miss, this man here is sitting in my seat!'

Frank made a display of getting out his boarding card: 'Three C? The seat number is three C? On my boarding card it says three C as well?' The ribaldry had an edge to it, because Aussie had always given Frank a hard time for his speaking abilities. 'First rule of politics, Aussie,' some cruel fellow called out, 'find a seat and hang onto it!' Aussie was shown the door. But at least the plane was still on the ground. Frank had gone to some trouble to get the booking clerk at the airline to double-book the seat deliberately. And flights were so heavily booked in those days he reckoned correctly that Aussie wouldn't get home until midday the day after.

In some sense you'd call this way of running things, Third World. In another sense you'd say: 'If only it were.' I remember Cecil, a friend of mine in Fiji. He was an electrician on one of the far-flung islands, and I helped get him a sort of internship with the Auckland power board to upgrade his skills. Or as he said, to put a bit of metropolitan know-how into his happy-go-lucky South Sea work habits. They gave him some wiring diagrams to sort out on his first morning and he took until morning tea to finish the work. That embarrassed the supervisor. (It was supposed to be a week's work.) 'Don't tell anyone,' was the supervisor's advice to Cecil. When they went out to re-install a transformer, things got worse. He watched twelve men work all day taking out one transformer and putting another in. He didn't want to tell them how he did the same job but eventually it came out. He took out the transformers and reinstalled them with four men in half a day. Curiosity got the better of them and he showed them how it was done. One man on an island with nothing but the manual to learn from had out-performed the entire Auckland power board. 'Don't tell anyone,' was the advice.

Politicians are naturally, fundamentally, and instinctively bad at running businesses because they have no incentive to run the businesses well. Their priorities are wrong. Why? Their first priority is control. That's very different from having a first priority of commercial success, or of delivering a first-rate service, or of fulfilling a need.

When I went along to buy my first house, I needed a

bridging loan. The bank only lent two-thirds of the value of the property. My bank manager had me in his office to inform me affectionately that he'd love to give me the loan, but the regulations (which he waved in front of me) forbade it. I asked to have a look at them. It was a full page of clauses called things like 18 3.1 (i) and (ii). The government was determining by regulation what the interest rate was, whom the banks could lend to, how much they could lend, what ratio of value to loan they could go up to, and what the lending priorities should be . . . hang on! 'It says here,' I pointed out, 'first-home buyers are actually your top priority.'

He cleared his throat and gave me the loan. Nobody had ever asked to see the regulations before, and he – like every other bank manager in the country – had been referring customers to the bank's finance house where the same loans were available for half as much again. That's how the industry got around the regulations, and how the government made everyone worse off in the process.

Today, the government's regulatory energies have been transferred into the health and safety sector. While I agree whole-heartedly that we need health and safety regulations, I believe we need health and safety regulations that work. I was chatting to a Christchurch roofer about a warehouse we were putting up. He said he wasn't allowed to work when the wind was thirty kilometres an hour or above. It was a national regulation. Sometimes the wind in Christchurch blows like that for a month. 'How do you run your business when that happens?' I asked.

He said: 'I do the smaller domestic jobs that the safety inspectors don't bother inspecting.'

'Isn't it dangerous?'

'Safer,' he said. 'I've been doing it for eighteen years and my father has before me. When you've got a steady wind you can lean the iron into it and it's easier to work with. You wouldn't want to work in places where the breeze comes and goes, but this steady wind makes ideal roofing conditions.' But there we are, we have a national regulation, and these local people in local conditions have no right to work in the way that experience tells them is safe.

This kind of blanket bureaucracy-by-the-book can be more dangerous than anything else. Safety has nothing to do with wearing a red vest; it's to do with whether you've been trained properly. Now, a lot of men hate wearing those red vests, and not just because they're ugly and hot, but because they don't do any good. A company I know analysed all their accidents and found that wearing a red vest would have prevented not one single accident. It brings to mind that Russian guarding the Tsar's children.

> This kind of blanket bureaucracy-by-the-book can be more dangerous than anything else.

Here's the reason for it. It has nothing to do with real safety. When you're an SOE director, your main nervousness is not profitability, service levels or product quality. No, it's being sued by Occupational Safety and Health (OSH) for half a million dollars. You do everything to prevent that. You are personally liable, and you can't insure yourself against OSH prosecution. Also, don't forget you're getting paid a twentieth amount of the possible penalty so the incentives are clear. The way to protect yourself is to have the organisation write a manual describing in minute and prescriptive detail how every single task related to the work should be completed (tea making falls under hot-water management). It doesn't stop accidents but it demonstrates your lively concern about these matters to the court.

This sort of bureaucratic thinking can go right across industry – public and private sectors both. It's worse in the public sector because everything moves more slowly and because the political masters come and go. Sometimes things move extra slowly because they are waiting for a political master to move on (it's happened to me, but we'll come to that in due course).

At the start of the reform process (and it's a surprise to remember it wasn't much more than twenty years ago), bureaucrats had no incentive to be efficient. The general manager of New Zealand Rail, when it was losing one million dollars a day, was the third highest paid civil servant. Why? Because he had so many staff. The more he employed, the more he was paid. If some general manager had reduced staff to a third and doubled the freight being carried at lower rates, a pay cut would have been his reward.

While politicians gave out free phones to win votes, the staff captured most of the benefits. Post office employees held over twenty thousand free phones. Then, because it was not fair to lose this perk just because you didn't work for the company any more, free phones were given to employees when they retired. All these free staff phones were not legal as civil service pay and conditions were decided by 'determinations'. There had never been a determination to grant staff free phones. The bureaucrats just gave it to themselves.

And who were we to object? We MPs had given ourselves free phones, free toll calls, free travel (and let's not go into the pension arrangements).

Since I could see that state ownership was not working to help the citizen, I gave a lot of thought to the reasons. It was all to do with the incentives. I tell the story of my neighbour who lived in a state house. He neglected it and let his children play ball inside. Then I noticed he had become house proud and was sending his children over to my yard to play ball. When I enquired as to the reason for this transformation, I learnt he had bought his house.

Incentives rule in the long term and very often in the short term as well. Owners have more incentive than renters. The politicians' incentive is to win votes. The bureaucrats, who propose the rules, have as their incentive to make more and more rules that require more and more bureaucrats.

But someone always pays. There are no free lunches, and there are no free phones. Free-phone calls go into the cost of the product. The country as a whole pays a big cost for these perks, red tape and bureaucracy. But here is the catch. We each pay only a small cost. The granting of

> Incentives rule in the long term and very often in the short term as well.

privileges has a small electoral cost but a big pay-off.

Politicians who make decisions for the general welfare are never popular because each citizen benefits so little. The real benefits of most of the changes I was responsible for arrived long after I had left office.

On the other hand, those who lose privileges such as subsidies or import licenses feel the loss immediately and acutely.

The ministers before me who had failed to reform knew this. As Machiavelli observed, there is nothing more dangerous than being a reformer. Those who benefit are not grateful and those who lose never forgive. To take the long view, you have to do things for posterity. But as Addison said nearly two hundred years ago, 'What's posterity ever done for me?'

So my belief in what government can do has faded with experience. I think governments try to do too much and as a result do nothing well. This is not to say government is not important. The recent history of the world has seen an amazing increase in prosperity that has reached all of society. This prosperity does not come from government programmes or aid. The prosperity comes from governments providing a

> The prosperity comes from governments providing a stable secure environment where individual enterprise can flourish.

stable secure environment where individual enterprise can flourish.

The answer is to limit government to doing those things that can only be done collectively, like running defence, law and order and a justice system. When you draw up the list of things that only the government can do, it is a long list. Many tasks, like limiting monopolies and promoting safety, are intrinsically difficult. With such difficult tasks to perform, it is folly for government to also take on tasks that citizens can do better. Let individual citizens make as many decisions as possible about their lives. Yes, some will make mistakes but at least they will be their mistakes. And to them, it may not be a mistake.

I used to think that government was wise and could make good decisions for people. My close-up experience of government has convinced me it cannot make good decisions for you. To government you are just a name and a tax number. Government does not even begin to know as much about you as you do.

As my faith in government has dwindled, my faith in people and their ability to invest, save and spend their own money to the advantage of their family, business and community has increased.

I think most of us in the Lange Labour Government had a similar journey. Some adults are not confident enough to honestly review what they believe against reality. Even worse are those Labour MPs who no longer believe in the state owning businesses; I include the present minister of finance, Michael Cullen and Prime Minister Helen Clark. The Labour Government opposes privatisation not because it is wrong,

> **Follow the incentives. If the incentive for everyone is for the project to succeed, then you have a winner.**

but because it is electorally unpopular.

Follow the incentives. If the incentive for everyone is for the project to succeed, then you have a winner.

As a student I worked in the freezing works. If the floor was not cleared by knock-off time, we received overtime. If we worked one minute of overtime we got paid for an hour and a half. Every day we failed to finish on time and then, miraculously, the work was done in minutes.

Failure

HUMAN SYNERGISTICS DID not always work. There are some problems beyond rational or managerial logic.

Following the 1987 share-market crash, the Cabinet had agreed to a series of measures to restore confidence and growth. The most important of these all was a low, flat tax of twenty-three cents in the dollar. It still creates a small shock when you run it through your mind. A top rate of income tax of twenty-three cents? Yes, it gets the heart going, that one.

We had worked through the issues, torture-tested the logic, drawn on our experience from the first term and come to the conclusion that this was the best and maybe the only way to revitalise the economy in the long term. It was another world-first in economics. It was a bold, strong, positive reaction and would build prosperity for a generation. The measures were all agreed by the Cabinet (which included some junior members who are senior Cabinet members today).

David Lange was making supportive noises. Fears that we'd had were assuaged by David's enthusiastic private endorsement of the project. He agreed the new flat tax should be set at twenty-three cents – but he refused to agree to the

Geoffrey Palmer, David Caygill, Michael Cullen, David Lange, Michael Bassett, me and Roger Douglas. Announcing the flat tax package, 1987. (*New Zealand Herald/APN*)

announcement of the parallel policy – a guaranteed family income for full-time workers to be set at eighty dollars above what that worker would have been eligible to receive on the dole. It was the punch line, he declared. If he announced it, he could take ownership of the policy and more effectively promote flat tax. (As Muldoon had frozen all wages, but benefits were indexed to the Consumer Price Index, this was a significant policy. Many rail workers would have been better off on the dole.)

So flat tax was announced (but not the guaranteed family income) and got a good reaction from the media and the public. I went off to Fiji for my holiday.

The next I heard was the prime minister, acting on his

own initiative, had cancelled it. 'It's time for a cup of tea,' he said, jokingly. David Lange knew the media liked his jokes but that the public didn't. Polling told him to keep his sense of humour under wraps. Obedient as he was to polling, he didn't make a joke for six months and his popularity was never higher. His unilateral announcement ripped up the doctrine of collective responsibility and made chimps of us. Everyone knows that was the moment the government started to split. I like to think I could have spotted it earlier; hindsight is a marvellous thing.

Rewind a few months, to the weeks after the share-market crash. The market was at rock bottom. New Zealand's market had fallen further than any other in the world. Part of the reason had been our deregulation in the early eighties. The country had behaved like convent schoolgirls released at the end of term. The share market went higher than anywhere else and fell lower. Some very good companies were being priced at less than the value of their assets.

We needed a circuit breaker to get things moving again. But what? Three years earlier we had halved income tax. The Left had been astounded to see that tax revenues increased as a result. Lower tax rates producing greater tax revenues? It didn't make sense. In fact it was a textbook example of the Laffer Curve in action. Two factors came into play. The first: it had become easier to pay tax than to pay tax specialists. The second: keeping more of your own profits encouraged investment (which encouraged growth, which produced a larger taxable base).

If cutting income tax from sixty-six cents to thirty-three cents had produced more tax revenue, what would happen if we cut the rate to twenty-three cents? It was this remarkable increase in revenue, which the Treasury computer model had not predicted, that made the Cabinet decide to adopt a low flat tax, a policy the prime minister had unilaterally cancelled.

That was the proposition we were still considering – the difficulty was that the finance minister and the prime minister weren't on speaking terms. They were writing each other letters from different parts of government buildings. Nothing was going to happen while that was the state of play.

I consulted with Michael Gourley. Could Human Synergistics help? He gave us the old marriage guidance advice: 'Yes, but only if the parties really want to resolve their differences.'

So I went to see the prime minister. David Lange said he did not want to discuss matters directly with Roger, one to one. Roger was such a formidable intellect I understood this. David had complained to me in the past that Roger always had a plan, and whenever they met, they inevitably ended up discussing it. David never had a plan of his own so the meetings ended up very one-sided.

I had explained to Michael Gourley that Lange would be reluctant to work directly with Douglas. The tensions in the government weren't common knowledge at that stage, but Michael didn't seem surprised at the news; having the two most powerful people in an organisation fall out isn't uncommon. Michael had a question: 'Does the Cabinet actually want to resolve the issues?'

'Every minister knows a rift would destroy the government, plunge the country into turmoil and result in them losing

FAILURE

their jobs, so the answer to your question is, yes.'

'If what you're saying is true we can work it out with the whole Cabinet in a day.' Michael said. I took the proposal back to the prime minister. He agreed, if Roger and the Cabinet agreed.

Roger told me he was willing to try anything. The Cabinet agreed. The outlook was good. Everyone was in agreement. But then why were we disagreeing? In retrospect the answer is easy. We weren't considering all the available facts.

We didn't think it would be a good look for the Cabinet to go on a retreat with a facilitator so we arranged for Michael to come secretly to a Monday Cabinet meeting. We would despatch the most urgent business quickly and then have a session with him.

I don't think this has ever been tried anywhere in the world, in any parliamentary democracy, mature or otherwise. At a pivotal moment in the socio-economic development of the country, a government Cabinet met, in government time, to give itself over to a morning of group therapy.

The session went well. The government collapsed afterwards, but the session went well. Human Synergistics wasn't to blame for the collapse; there were some very deep problems we had, deeper even than Michael could reach. Mind you, the problems he could reach were quite enough to be going on with.

He got us to do our self-assessment profiles. While Michael has never revealed any individual score to me, this is where he learnt that the cabinet had one of the highest achieving profiles his company had ever surveyed anywhere in the world.

He began by giving us the test for placing us on the spectrum for sensory/intuitive thinking.

Sensories are people for whom, if they cannot touch, see or smell an object, it does not exist. They are practical people. They do a lot of the world's work. Most engineers are sensories. Intuitives are people who can visualise things that do not exist and maybe never will. Most architects are intuitives.

Intuitives and sensories usually do not get on. Sensories think intuitives are impractical, dreamers and liars. Intuitives think that sensories are stupid, insensitive and blind to the possibilities. The two groups often talk past each other, not understanding what the other is saying. Of course, most balanced people have a mixture of sensory and intuitive thinking but we all operate best (or if not best, then mostly) in one mode or another. Some people are very high in one style and have almost none of the other. They can be very high achievers but they certainly need support in the areas where they are deficient.

The conservative National Party was high in sensory thinking and the Labour Party was equally high in intuitive thinking. Bill Birch, the architect of the disastrous Think Big heavy engineering projects, every one of which failed, is a sensory. You could see him thinking 'How can so much concrete be wrong?' Sensories often appear to be highly competent. Sir Robert Muldoon was a sensory. He felt he could solve any crisis – as he often could. Tactically he was brilliant, but he had no strategy. Each solution – price controls, for example – only temporally solved the problem but in the end made it worse.

Intuitives, on the other hand, are more strategic in their thinking. Often they are impractical. The Sydney Opera House is a wonderful concept but its architect did not know how to build it.

It is interesting to think that the Left/Right split in politics can be explained by the way we think: intuitively or practically. Human Synergistics' latest research casts some doubt on this analysis but I think there is no doubt that there is a lot of truth in it.

David Lange was an intuitive. But the split between Roger and David cannot be explained as an intuitive/sensory division because the survey showed that Sir Roger was also an intuitive. He is one of those rare individuals high in both intuitive and sensory thinking. How many visionary accountants do you know?

We went into the discussion about the circuit breaker. We laid out the facts we had assembled. We did a card sort, giving propositions to different people to argue, we got the ideas up, we separated them from personalities, and we were steaming ahead. It was such an intellectually stimulating morning that it took some time before we realised something was wrong. Something was very, very wrong. We realised David Lange wasn't in the room.

David often left Cabinet, caucus and other meetings. He had a low boredom threshold, and found conflict distressing. He also used to slip out to have a fag. So when he slipped out we were not at first concerned. It was Michael Bassett who noticed the prime minister wasn't there. We had a discussion about how long he had been gone. We tried to work out his last contribution and calculated he had been gone for more than forty minutes. We realised that David Lange was not coming back.

That was it. That was the moment. It wasn't anything said or done; the end of it all was an absence. It was an absence at the heart of the government where there had once been a relationship; it was an absence that gathered significance until it became the single most important thing about us.

There at the time a number of us dimly recognised the seriousness of it. We wondered if we should go and look for him. It is not a good look for ministers to come out of Cabinet asking 'Has anyone seen the prime minister?' We concluded there was no point.

FAILURE

David Lange and Roger Douglas – the rift becomes obvious. (*New Zealand Herald/APN*)

In my view, the reasons for the split were all too human and all too common. A certain sort of confidential information at the time used to come my way and it formed my view of what the deep-down problem was.

We polled a lot, as governments do, and the pollsters would report directly to David Lange after which the results would be circulated to the inner Cabinet, and sometimes beyond. There came a time when Lange started to suppress some of the results – particularly those relating to himself and those relating to Roger. What David didn't know was

BUT I'LL BE BACK...

(*New Zealand Herald/APN*)

that the pollsters had me in the loop earlier than him – not for intelligence reasons, just so that I could cast a professional eye over the questions and methodology. So when David circulated the results I knew what wasn't there. It's a very bad sign, suppressing poll results you don't like. It's the first evasion of reality; it's the start of culture beginning to rot.

And what was so upsetting that it had to be hidden? Here we come to it; this is base reality underlying so much of our endeavours.

David found he was the most popular member of the government – and the most unpopular. He polarised opinion. You liked him or loathed him. And the fact that he was overwhelmingly popular didn't help. Because Roger Douglas was not only widely liked – he wasn't loathed at all. I told

FAILURE

David: 'People think there's no point in hating Roger. They don't kick their calculators across the room either.' It cut no ice with David. I think, for their first years in collaboration, David didn't consider Roger a politician at all. He was the bean counter you had to have. He was the finance director you were expected to have in the line up. But suddenly here he was a symbol of the government. Suddenly it was the Lange/Douglas Government. Then to some it was Rogernomics and the Roger Douglas Government.

And more than that, David found the flat-tax plan threatening because he fully realised how significant it was. It had the power to create a new sort of society. It was such a big story that Roger might have written that David feared history's judgement might not leave any room for him.

The party slowly, inexorably turned back to what it was before Human Synergistics had become involved – rife with faction and personality-driven differences.

As a group we were higher in achievement thinking than any in the world at the time. Even a group like that couldn't face the reality that it had to sack the prime minister or the finance minister or both of them. It shows how hard it is to face facts that we wish weren't true.

It's culture that counts

HUMAN SYNERGISTICS' RESEARCH discloses that success is all down to culture. The research shows there are a number of leadership styles that produce good results, depending on the circumstances. The power style can be dramatically successful when circumstances respond to drama. The fatal flaw of the power culture is handling change. It doesn't handle change very well.

The very style which has brought success, prevents the organisation from being able to change. Take the famous power statement: 'When the going gets tough, the tough get going.'

Something is wrong; the reaction is to keep on doing what you have been doing but harder and faster. Sometimes it works; often it makes you fail faster. If you're in a hole, remember the first Law of Holes (stop digging).

Many businessmen have a power style. IBM, the computer giant, was built on it. The 1950s reacted well to power styles, when people did what they were told to do. The black-suit-white-shirt uniform put a value on conformity when conformity was valued. But then came the sixties and seventies. Individualism was everywhere. But IBM's reasoning stayed the same: 'Big computers will always beat the little ones'. A power thinker could not imagine the personal computer being the future.

The paradox is that power thinking often leads to passive organisation.

As minister of police I was very impressed with the New Zealand police force. New Zealand police have high integrity, a clear sense of duty and a keen desire to uphold the rule of law. As an organisation they believe in order, structure, duty.

Their fundamental values made them very slow to adapt to new situations.

I can remember when doing accounting as a student, in the preface in my textbook there was a short description of single-entry accounting. The author said that single-entry accounting did not show the true value of a firm and so had been replaced by double-entry accounting. Not in government.

The New Zealand Government was still doing single-entry accounting in the 1980s. This meant that the government had no idea of the value of its assets, what return it was receiving from its investments or the true value of its spending. No allowance was made for depreciation, so the government did not know what its liabilities were.

The businessmen whom I appointed to the government businesses were horrified to discover that departments didn't even keep proper assets registers and so had no idea what they owned. This is typical of a culture that is passive and defensive.

The first task of all the new boards was to do an inventory of what they owned. What they discovered astonished everyone concerned.

New Zealand Post appointed some consultants armed with clipboards to record the corporation's assets. One consultant was sent to a large post office warehouse in the Hutt Valley. The warehouse covered hectares. What he found was hundreds of thousands of old black dial telephones that were still recorded in the books at the original value. At the back of the warehouse he discovered a huge packing case, the size of a room.

'What's in there?' he asked the foreman.

'I don't know,' replied the foreman. 'It's been there all the time I've worked here.'

'Who is the longest-serving employee?' asked the consultant. The answer was old Joe, who was summoned. He too had always wondered what was in the packing case.

To the horror of the staff the consultant took a crow bar and attacked the case. What they found was a brand new 1930s Bedford truck. They put petrol in the engine, turned the crank lever and the motor started. But for the flat tyres they could have driven it back to the dealer for a refund. It was probably worth quite a lot of money: a vintage truck in mint condition and nothing on the clock; it might even have fetched the cost of its fifty-year storage.

The police department could not see why it needed to move to double-entry accounting. I tried in vain to explain it would give us much better knowledge of the organisation's financial health. I became suspicious that the department didn't want to know.

IT'S CULTURE THAT COUNTS

I insisted we switch to double-entry accounting and discovered that there was a huge multi-million dollar unfunded liability for overtime. The police department didn't pay overtime. What they did was to grant days off in lieu. Some staff had years owing to them. In effect, the department was overspending its budget each year but this didn't show on the books.

You can easily forgive these practical chaps for keeping out of the way of double-entry bookkeeping, but they were also slow to adopt new technology or to adapt to new trends in crime.

At the time, Auckland was being hit by a series of daring daytime raids on suburban banks. The police would be called, but by the time they arrived the robbers had escaped. The robbers invariably used a stolen vehicle for the robbery, which they quickly dumped and then transferred into another vehicle and disappeared into traffic.

The bank robberies made front-page news, lead items on television and quickly created the impression of lawlessness.

I said to the commissioner of police, 'What we need is a helicopter.' The police hierarchy was totally opposed to

(*New Zealand Herald/APN*)

the idea. While on a trip to the United States I arranged to stop off in Los Angeles to travel on a Los Angeles Police Department (LAPD) helicopter to see for myself how such helicopters work.

It was a night patrol. The pilots were both police officers who were every bit as world-weary and tough as in any Hollywood movie. What Hollywood does not betray was the scream of crime that came over the police radio. Shootings, robberies, drive-by killings, muggings and burglaries just poured out. The pilots explained that they operated independently, listened to the police radio and followed up reports of crime where they thought they could assist. I asked why they had ignored a reported drive-by shooting in the suburb where we were flying. The answer was it would take three minutes to get there and how would we find the car?

He had a good point. At night from a helicopter, LA looks like a crisscross of bright white lines made by millions of car lights, and stretching as far as you can see. At sixty miles an hour, in three minutes the car has gone three miles. This was a limitation of a helicopter.

Then came a report of officers in pursuit of a stolen car. Our helicopter went immediately to join the pursuit. Talking on the radio with the police car we soon located the fleeing vehicle. There was no way the car could escape. The helicopter's night/sun searchlight blindingly lit up the vehicle and we brought the car to a halt.

I was interested in how cautiously the officers handled the arrest. No officer approached the car but they drew their guns and crouched down behind their cars and asked the offender to first show them his hands. The offender was ordered to go slowly around the car opening the doors and was then ordered to lie flat with his hands out in front of him. The officers cautiously checked the car for any other occupant and only then rushed the offender, quickly handcuffing him.

From the helicopter I could smell their fear. It was nothing like the arrests one sees on TV or that I had witnessed in New Zealand.

Discussing it with my police companions, they explained that many people arrested in LA are high on drugs and very dangerous. One of the pilots said that two of his partners had been shot dead, that's why he flew a helicopter.

We went to half a dozen crime scenes during the night and each time, once we had located the offender, there was no way he could escape. While the police commissioner told me police dogs could replicate some of the captures, I reckoned a helicopter came out of the comparison better, at least for high-speed car chases.

Eventually I persuaded New Zealand Police to hire one for a trial. It took only a week to catch the bank robbers and that was when that sort of police work changed. Whenever the police helicopter brings me out of a deep sleep, I've only myself to blame. As an aside, it turned out all the bank robbers were on the taxpayers' payroll. Sir Robert Muldoon had been persuaded that a way to deal with gangs was to put them on work schemes so they could learn good work

Never pay for what you do not want more of.

habits. They were very hard-working young men, but at bank robbery. Never pay for what you do not want more of.

I was not minister of police long enough to achieve a change in culture. I did ask Michael Gourley if Human Synergistics had done any work with police. He produced for me a remarkable study on policing in Harlem.

It was a study on who made the most effective patrolmen. American police always patrol in twos. Was it two young, fit white males (as we were recruiting in New Zealand)? Was it two young black men? Was it two older police? Or was it two women? The Americans tried all combinations.

The least successful combination was a white man and a white woman. The man tried to upstage the woman or protect her, and in the course of both activities was extremely prone to shooting people.

The combinations of two young white men, two young black men and a white and a black young male were a little more successful. But for various reasons, they were involved in constant confrontations.

IT'S CULTURE THAT COUNTS

Older patrolmen had fewer confrontations. But the most successful combination was two middle-aged black women. During the whole trial in crime-ridden Harlem, they never had to draw their guns. They managed to keep the peace and reduce crime without confrontations with the public.

The reason, the report concluded, was psychological. Young men do most of the crime. Males are psychologically trained from birth to obey their mothers. When a woman who looks like their mother says, 'Don't do that', young men obey. When an older male gives the same order his age gives him some authority but the young male will naturally seek to challenge the older male. A young man giving the same order creates a challenge. But a couple of pleasant middle-aged women! Forget the guns and the car chases and the body armour!

To tell a macho organisation like the police that their mothers could do their job better than they could ... it was an uphill assignment. The police had a policy of early retirement and selecting young fit men. There were no middle-aged Maori policewomen. The few women there were, were young, and most of them married policemen and left the force. All I managed was to get the age of recruitment lifted so that people could join at an older age.

> To tell a macho organisation like the police that their mothers could do their job better than they could ... it was an uphill assignment.

One question I asked is, 'What do police do?' The answer was revealing: 'Keep the peace,' they said.

'Oh really? The public thinks you are fighting crime,' I ventured. No, no, no. The commissioner strongly disagreed. In his view, crime was the result of societal pressures and all the police could do was maintain order depending on what order there was to maintain.

In effect, police were saying that crime was the community's responsibility, not theirs. Most senior police were convinced that the police force could do nothing to lower the incidence of crime. The causes of crime were societal, such as bad parenting. This is nonsense.

When the commissioner had got over his shock of having a minister who read research into policing, he brought me some interesting data from England. At that time, when the pubs closed at 11 p.m., pub closing time was the busiest for police. Drunken patrons came out of hotels and got into fights with the police.

When the police were withdrawn from all over London to combat the Brixton riots they feared that there would be a crime wave at 11 p.m. What actually happened was that crime went down. The inebriated patrons came out of the pubs looking for police to fight. When they couldn't find them, they simply decided to go home.

We had an élite squad of police in Wellington made up of the biggest officers – rugby players and the like. They would patrol Wellington hotels. There were a high number of arrests, which seemed to prove that they were needed.

The commissioner sought my approval to disband the squad. This was politically unpopular but my public prediction that the crime rate would fall turned out to be correct. Arrests in Wellington fell spectacularly.

I supported New Zealand Police advising the sellers of liquor that they were responsible for order in their establishments. They could not keep selling their patrons liquor until they were so drunk and disorderly that they had to call the police. On being told that most trouble came from the same few hotels, I asked, 'Why don't the police oppose the badly run establishments from being reissued with liquor licences?'

The police almost never opposed relicensing applications. They said to me that such action would be unpopular. Egged on by me, they did oppose a number of applications, and one was refused. The effect on the industry was electric. Problems in hotels dropped so much that the police were able to further reduce hotel patrolling.

One example of the importance of analysing the problem was the sudden crime wave in Hastings. The local commander in Hastings began a campaign in his local newspaper for more police officers. Headlines appeared saying things like 'Crime up 20 per cent', 'Police overwhelmed by crime wave.' The paper called for more police.

I got head office to send me the raw police data for Hastings. What I saw was that reported crime had not gone up; what had risen dramatically was arrests. When I analysed the arrests, the big rise was for underage drinking, assaults on police and resisting arrest. Many offenders were being multiply charged.

The drinking age was twenty. Any police officer could have gone into any hotel and arrested a number of patrons for underage drinking. In a university pub half of the patrons were underage.

When we put the problem on the whiteboard, it was easy to see what was causing the crime wave. The police chief was looking for crime and had caused a crime wave.

Were there really more crimes being committed than the year before? It's like the question: 'How many kinds of beetle are there?' The question has a theoretical answer – but the reality is, the longer you look, the more kinds of beetle you find.

I told the commissioner that I thought he should let the Hastings commander know that the minister of police was so impressed with him that I had recommended he be transferred to Ruatoria. I had no power to transfer any officer anywhere but the Rastafarians were causing mayhem on the East Coast and just the thought of being transferred there was enough. The crime wave in Hastings came to an immediate stop.

The police were not used to having a minister examine raw crime data. What I was looking for was what worked. The police, who believe crime is caused by complicated social factors, didn't believe anything they did would reduce crime and so didn't look for solutions.

I believe we discovered 'zero tolerance for crime' policing before commissioner Grantham pioneered it in New York. I asked police in South Auckland, 'Why is crime in this neighbourhood so much lower than in its identical surrounding neighbourhoods? What are we doing differently?'

The only difference, they said, was that the local neighbourhood policeman in the precinct hated graffiti and was

IT'S CULTURE THAT COUNTS

cracking down on it. This will remind readers of the well-known story of commissioner Grantham, the sometime police commissioner of the New York subway system. The trains were hotbeds of crime. Muggings and murders were common. A significant number of patrons would skip over the turnstiles and not pay.

Grantham instructed his subway police to arrest turnstile jumpers. Not only did turnstile jumping stop but also, to his surprise, all crime in the subway system fell.

So he asked his police to arrest for other minor offences they had been ignoring like graffiti and littering. All crime in the subway system fell even further. He was then made the New York police commissioner. New York City was rotten with crime. And now it's not. Grantham had made this fundamental discovery: if you clean up minor crime, you reclaim the area and all crime falls.

The courts also played a part. I watched a court in Manhattan where offenders arrested the previous night (and in one case arrested that morning) were arraigned, convicted and sentenced that day. Offenders arrested in New Zealand on New Year's day might not be sentenced until July. To an eighteen-year-old, six months is a lifetime.

In New York an effort is made for sentences to be public and appropriate. Those convicted for littering were made to wear bright orange overalls and were required to go out onto the streets and clean up where the previous night they had littered.

As I say, we could have introduced 'zero tolerance for crime' in New Zealand. We had the data. Why didn't I just order the police to crack down on graffiti? Partly because the law barred me, as minister, from telling the police whom to arrest. That's a police state. But also because just issuing orders is a management style that doesn't work. I did issue the police with an order and I believe it was my biggest failure as minister.

> Just issuing orders is a management style that doesn't work.

I said, 'You have not told me what police do. How does a constable spend his time?' Police headquarters did not know. I got them to do a time-and-motion study and it revealed that the average constable spent 22 per cent of his time typing out reports.

Despite spending so much of their day typing, most police laboriously typed with two fingers.

My response to the survey was to suggest that all police should be able to touch type and to make it a prerequisite for entry. 'Most of these reports must be standard. We should give every constable a word processor to increase their efficiency.'

The police responded to my suggestion with the news that they needed some personal computers for the Incis computer project. The biggest waste of money on any computer project in New Zealand's history.

Incis was envisaged as a computer program to process every task the New Zealand Police undertake. 'It will be world class, leading edge, a world-first.' All words that are warning signals of an impending computer disaster. The police explained that no other police service in the world had

IT'S CULTURE THAT COUNTS

such a computer program. Incis would enable a policeman to note down a car registration number and the name and criminal record of the driver would instantly appear, together with the description of the driver. If the car was stopped the constable would be able to note down some details of the driver – height, weight, eye colour – and the computer would do a scan to find a match.

Incis offered, I could see, a dream list of everything police had ever wished for. Indeed, that's how the specs had been put together.

I also noted that each officer had to log in from the moment they started work and record what they were doing all day. It was very reminiscent of 'big brother is watching you'. Head office always wanted to know what the troops were up to. This computer would be akin to giving officers their own 'black box'. In the event of a complaint, senior officers could go back and review all the constable's actions. Defence lawyers would love it.

> 'It will be world class, leading edge, a world-first.' All words that are warning signals of an impending computer disaster.

If I could see that Incis was a head-office spy, the police on the beat could also see this feature. It would never work. The constables on the streets would make sure it did not work. 'Rubbish in, rubbish out.'

I summoned the senior team together and took a morning

to explain why their computer project would fail. I told them of the computer disasters that I had seen in other departments. 'It will cost a fortune and it will never work, if only because the beat constables can see this is for head office and not what they need.'

'There are six hundred police forces in America that are bigger than entire New Zealand Police. Americans computerise everything. If they have not developed a program like this, the reason is because it cannot be done.

'Go back and ask the constables what they need! I bet they'd find it more useful to have their own PCs. You can buy them off the shelf.' I suggested. 'And what's more you know they'll work!'

The police said 'Yes minister' and did the opposite. It is one of my biggest failures. I thought I had persuaded the police that the Incis computer project was a bad idea. What I had really done was issue an order not to buy it. They knew there would be a change of government in a few months and they simply put the proposition to the new minister. The project took seven years, over ninety million dollars and had to be abandoned as unworkable.

IT'S CULTURE THAT COUNTS

It is an example of power thinking. Such a big computer had to be good. Some cause-and-effect thinking would have produced very different priorities.

As I say, the police passed the 'causes of crime' buck on to society. The other organisation that believes this profoundly negative idea is even more influential in our national life. In fact, it is so influential that it is fundamental to the way our culture is created.

The teachers' orthodoxy has it that school success is more or less entirely dependent on the home life of the parents of their students. That's convenient, if you wanted to absolve yourself of all responsibility in educational outcomes.

It's nonsense, and it's dangerous nonsense. Try telling parents keen to enrol their children at desirable schools that schooling makes no difference. A study by Rutter that follows pupils from sociologically identical neighbourhoods in London, called *Fifteen Thousand Hours* (the amount of time pupils in England must compulsorily spend schooling), proved schooling makes a huge difference.* The worst pupils at the best schools did better than the best pupils from the worst schools. And the difference? It was not class size, buildings, whether the school was co-ed or single sex, or any of the things we are told that matter, but what the author called the school's 'ethos'. It's what I've been calling 'culture'. Rutter's study found that the source of the ethos was usually very simple: the principal.

---

* Michael Rutter, *Fifteen Thousand Hours: Secondary Schools and their Effects on Children* (Cambridge, MA: Harvard University Press, 1982).

For what it's worth, I've found what Rutter says to be invariably correct.

When a bad principal joins a good school it only takes him or her a term to ruin the school. When a good principal joins a bad school it takes two years to turn the school around. Four months to send a school to the bad, twenty-four months to bring it back.

The first sign of the change is teachers leaving. Good teachers are readily employable and leave within a term of the appointment of a bad principal. Bad teachers are not so employable and it takes time for a good principal to remove them.

I believe I can assess a school from the journey from where I park my car to reaching the principal's office. Here are two examples.

Newton Central school. When I was first elected MP for Auckland Central, Newton Central was a ghetto. The school role was 96 per cent Pacific Island. Over half the school roll had appeared in the children's court in the past year. A new principal was appointed. He was, I recall, from Napier and believed the pupils were no worse than those in the school he had left. 'White flight'

IT'S CULTURE THAT COUNTS

Being interviewed by a child on a school visit.

meant he had an empty classroom available so he decided to teach a class of civics himself.

He was convinced that much of the trouble was cultural. So he taught pupils how to ask if they could pick apples from a tree instead of stealing them. The programme was so successful that within a year the offending rate for pupils of his school was lower than for those from up-market Remuera Intermediate. So the education board declared the programme a success and the classroom surplus to requirements, and scheduled its removal. I was called in.

I recall the school had clearly marked visitors parking. A little girl and boy were waiting for me. 'My name is Mary,' 'My name is Tua,' they said. 'We are welcoming visitors to Newton Central school this week'. There was a large sign saying "Welcome". They escorted me to the principal's office. The grounds, I noticed, were tidy. They both told me how much they loved school. By the time I reached the principal's office I knew it was a good school. He greeted me enthusiastically and insisted on taking me on a tour and telling me of the school's ambitious plans.

In contrast to this was a visit to Western Springs High school. A visionary principal named Peters had made this working-class school a good one. Under his urging I had obtained many things for the school. A new principal was appointed and contact ceased. So I made an appointment to see the principal. When I arrived I could see nowhere to park my car, so parked out on the road. I could see no signs indicating the way to the principal's office. There were pupils aimlessly wandering the grounds and bits of paper blowing around.

I made a guess at the correct building and eventually found the principal's office. A harassed-looking secretary asked what I wanted. I explained that I had an appointment. 'Oh dear, the principal is not here.' The secretary clearly did not know what to do with me and suggested I might like to go to the staff room and make myself a cup of coffee. I received some complicated instructions and after walking down a number of corridors I found the staff room. There were two teachers looking like survivors of some catastrophe. I said hello and that I was the local MP. I explained the principal's office had suggested I come down and make myself a cup of coffee. The two just stared at me. No response to my greeting.

I decided to go about making myself a cup of coffee. I surveyed the cups. They had the permanent tea stains that

IT'S CULTURE THAT COUNTS

only repeated use without washing can generate. I guessed each teacher had his or her own stained cup. For reasons of hygiene, if nothing else, I sought some other utensil, found some plastic cups and made myself a cup of instant coffee. The two teachers and I then sat like strangers at an airport waiting for a flight we just know is going to be late.

Eventually the principal arrived. No explanation was offered. The next twenty minutes were spent listening to her complaining. No vision. No offer to show me anything about the school. No thanks for my considerable efforts for the school or even awareness of what I had done.

I recall we were constantly interrupted by requests. I could see the principal did not know the answer to the problems as she suggested they ask the dean, the caretaker or anyone else but her.

As I monitored that school, I saw it decline in every way. Its only achievement was to become a hotbed of union militancy. All educational problems were the government's fault and the universal answer to every problem was more money. The negative, avoidance culture of the school was pervasive.

Organisations with a culture of denial cannot make effective decisions. First they do not accept the reality that change is necessary. Secondly, even if the people in the organisation do not like the situation, and people in such organisations are usually unhappy, they do not believe their efforts will make any difference. They believe that things happen because of fate; somebody (not they) should do something; it's the government's fault; people who succeed do so because they are lucky; 'it's who you know' and they explain away their

> While I have met some successful people who claim to have been lucky, it is my experience that you make your own luck.

own failure because in some way successful people have cheated.

While I have met some successful people who claim to have been lucky, it is my experience that you make your own luck. 'The harder I work, the luckier I get,' as is sometimes said. Certainly, we all know of Lotto winners who have managed to fritter it all away. Having said that, I have to admit that I have been very lucky. Lucky to meet Mike Gourley. Very lucky to be in the extraordinary Lange Cabinet (my fellow ministers were always very supportive). I was lucky in ACT to be leading what commentators agreed was a very talented caucus. I have also been lucky to serve on boards with some of New Zealand's most able businessmen. So, except in my own case, I do not believe in luck.

The uselessness of audit

I SHOULD HAVE realised that something was wrong with the shipping corporation. On a visit to North America, the corporation insisted I meet with their wonderful American partners. I was in transit to Canada. The partners were to meet me at LAX, take me to lunch and return me in time for my flight.

On arrival I immediately noticed an Italian-American looking man, in a double-breasted pinstriped suit with a black shirt and white tie. I swear he was wearing spats.

He was holding a sign with my name on it and I noticed no one stood near him. I introduced myself. He said his name was Tony and led me to the longest car I have ever seen. It was parked in the red zone, about which a recorded message says, 'cars parked in the red zone will be towed away'. No one was touching this car. In the back seat there was a bar and room for a swimming pool. Our front wheels were leaving the airport while the back wheels were still in the red zone.

I was taken to the *Queen Mary* and introduced to two more men of Italian origin who spoke with strong New

Jersey accents. They also wore double-breasted suits, dark shirts and light ties. As they were in transport I attempted to discuss transport issues. I realised they knew even less than I did.

When I returned to New Zealand I asked the auditor general to see me. I told him I thought I had had lunch with the Mafia. I asked him to conduct a snap audit. He replied he was an independent officer and did not do audits just because a minister imagined he had met the Mafia. I thought he might say that so I gave him a letter setting out my suspicions and my recommendation. If events turned out as I thought, he could explain his lack of action.

I heard nothing more until Stan Roger, the minister in charge of the audit office, rang me one evening to ask if I had seen the report the auditor general was tabling in parliament the next day. 'You better have a look. You are being slammed. Apparently the mafia has stolen about eighteen million dollars from the shipping corporation.'

When I read the report it revealed that the shipping corporation's American partners were the Mafia and there were millions missing. The auditor held me responsible. How he must be savouring the sweetness of his revenge.

I summoned the auditor general. I asked him a series of four questions, three of which he answered.

'When was this contract signed?' Two years ago.

'How many audits have you done without discovering these thefts?' Three.

'When did I become the minister?' Eight months ago.

'Why did you do a snap audit?' That's when the answers gave out.

THE USELESSNESS OF AUDIT

'I kept a copy of the letter I gave you.' That wasn't a question. But the auditor general eventually volunteered a suggestion: 'Perhaps we should rewrite our report,' the independent official said. The new report no longer blamed me but neither did it mention my role in uncovering the fraud.

I have never found that auditors discover fraud. Nor have I found their style of thinking to be of much assistance to management. The real advantage of audit is to make sure we keep accounts!

I should have realised that the state-owned enterprise model by itself is no guarantee of success. The quality solution was privatisation. With no acceptance, could we have got it through?

> I have never found that auditors discover fraud. Nor have I found their style of thinking to be of much assistance to management.

Seeing ourselves

OUR VIEW OF ourselves and how others see us can be very different.

When I do the Human Synergistic leadership impact self-questionnaire I score very highly on achievement, self-actualising, humanistic-encouraging and affiliative. But then, I'm doing the marking.

People are classified into a number of different leadership styles.

- Self-actualising. Deals with issues objectively and honestly. Handles crisis situations well. Generates unique solutions to problems.
- Achievement. Anticipates future trends and opportunities. Takes reasonable and well-calculated risks. Takes initiative to get things done.
- Perfectionistic. Demands perfection. Sets unrealistically high goals.
- Competitive. Develops opponents rather than allies. Sees things in 'win–lose' terms.
- Power. Interested in gaining influence. Dictatorial.

- Oppositional. Quick to criticise. Quick to point out why an idea won't work.
- Avoidance. Procrastinates. Waits for problems to take care of themselves.
- Dependent. Depends on others for ideas. Prefers to follow rather than lead.
- Conventional. Achieves by conforming. Relies on past policies and strategies.
- Approval. Agrees too readily. Looks for solutions to please all.
- Affiliative. Gets co-operation through personal loyalties. Concern for others.
- Humanistic-encouraging. Encourages others to express their ideas. Promotes open discussion.*

I have always scored myself 100 per cent for achievement thinking. That's fair, after all. I give myself a medium score for competitive and power thinking; although it's true I have spent all my adult life in the competitive power world of politics. I can't explain that. Someone who spells as badly as I do can't be a perfectionist so I give myself a brutally low score for perfectionism. Although critics have claimed I am a good opposition politician, that seems to me to be rubbish and the result of sloppy thinking so I score myself low in opposition thinking; the aggressive/defensive styles.

In the passive/defensive styles of avoidance and approval I

---

* Researched and developed by Robert A Cooke and J Clayton Lafferty. © Copyright Human Synergistics International Ltd.

score a zero. I self-mark a very low score for being conventional and dependent.

I see myself as leading people to take on challenging tasks with a sense of confidence, setting personal goals and taking the initiative when opportunities arise.

As the Human Synergistics professionals explain, how you see yourself is not the important thing. It's more important how others see you.

When you do the leadership impact survey you often come up with a very different picture. The survey is given to those you report to, your peers and those who report to you. As the manual that accompanies the survey soothingly says,

'For most managers, there are some significant differences or "gaps" between their ideal impact profile and the profile showing their current impact on others.'

You can say that again. My leadership impact charts were shockingly different from my rosy self-assessment.

I have always said that to be a politician you need a big ego. It is not likely that you really are the best person to represent fifty-seven thousand people, the standard size of a New Zealand electorate, but that is not something that stops the average politician from being convinced he or she is that person.

I suppose this comes as no surprise to the public, but my leadership impact survey gave my principle style as aggressive/defensive, high in perfectionist and power behaviour. As a leader, I cause people to work long hours, focus on the task and view the work as more important than anything else. The survey said I lead people to act forcefully, aggressively assert themselves and stay on the offensive. You want to rise to my defence, I know, but I can only say that truth hurts.

As the leader of a party, I reported only to the board of ACT; my peers were my fellow MPs and those who reported to me were my parliamentary staff. So I asked three board members, three MPs and three staff members to complete the leadership impact reports on me.

What the survey showed was that my style for each group was different.

All three gave my primary style as perfectionist.

I was pleased to see all agreed that I was not passive, by giving me some zero scores for approval and conventional. If you seek approval as a politician you will be dead within a week of parliament and the media going after you.

I was also gratified to see that my own MPs gave me my own grading for self-actualising and a very high grade for achievement. They did not think I was as humanistic-encouraging as I did. My own staff were not hard on me. Not surprisingly, my staff gave me a score for dependent behaviour. I suspect that reflects my dependence on my personal secretary, without whose help I would never catch an aeroplane.

The 2005 ACT caucus.
Back Row: Gary Eckhoff, Stephen Franks, Deborah Coddington, Ken Shirley. *Front Row*: Kenneth Wong, Heather Roy, Rodney Hide, Muriel Newman, me.

It was the board members who gave me the very high score for power behaviour. On reflection, that would be their experience. There is, in any party, a tension between the parliamentary party and the board. As parliamentary leader I was always demanding resources and a focus on elections. I did not see it as part of my job to devote time to the personal development of board members.

I reflected on my survey results. Politics and business are not the same. Business is usually a win–win matter. People do not trade unless they expect to benefit. Most trades benefit both parties.

And almost all business ventures result in some measure of success. Total failure, as with total success, is not the norm. It is usually a matter of incremental improvement. You try something, if it works you persist; if it doesn't, you try something else.

In politics it's a matter of win–lose. There is just one 'sale day' every three years. Very few businesses bet the total house on one deal. There are very few business transactions where you totally win or you totally lose as you do on election day. I think that does make for power thinking in politics. It takes a certain personality to enjoy the gamble of politics.

I think that politicians, if they are to be successful in their different roles – a candidate for office, then an MP and then minister in charge of a department – do need to have the ability to switch from the aggressive style needed to win, to a more constructive style needed in government.

Having made those rationalisations, I had a hard think about my style. The handbook that accompanied my leadership impact report said, 'The most important force for change and

> Business is usually a win–win matter. People do not trade unless they expect to benefit.

> In politics it's a matter of win–lose. There is just one 'sale day' every three years. Very few businesses bet the total house on one deal.

> Those who are interested and motivated can effect important changes based on the feedback ... similarly those who lack motivation or interest are unlikely to experience any growth or development.

development is the recipient of the feedback. Those who are interested and motivated can effect important changes based on the feedback ... similarly those who lack motivation or interest are unlikely to experience any growth or development.'

Is that not the truth?

It is one of Murphy's many laws that keeping one's bad habits requires little effort, whereas learning new good habits requires real sustained effort. As the handbook put it: 'Moving towards a more prescriptive style, and having a more constructive impact on others, will require an investment of both time and effort.'

Achieving successful personal change is like any other successful turn-around. First you need a reality check. It is necessary to recognise that change is needed. Then you need to know in what direction the change must move, what style of behaviour to avoid and what to promote. In my experience, significant improvement is achievable. One can train oneself to be more constructive.

It is unfortunate that those who need it most are often

the most resistant. It has been my frequent experience that it is the good manager, who you would think needs no help, who is the keenest to improve their performance.

Organisational culture

HUMAN SYNERGISTICS' SURVEYS of managers in New Zealand and Australia find that most managers have a gap between the constructive style they know they should use to lead and the aggressive, negative style that their employees experience. Why is that?

Just as the environment of politics encourages power behaviour so we take our signals not from the mission statements but from what we observe to be the real culture of the firm.

First we shape our buildings and then they shape us. First we shape our jobs then they shape us.

The railway guards were regarded even by their own union as unemployable. When I inspected a guard's van I noticed that the guard's chair could fold right out to be almost a bed.

ORGANISATIONAL CULTURE

The management explained that the guards were encouraged to sleep on the job as then they caused less trouble. No matter how well a guard carried out the few duties he had, he could never be promoted. No wonder they caused trouble. The crash firemen were never consulted about their equipment or vehicles. Was it a surprise that when an aeroplane crashed on the mudflats the hovercraft was out of order?

The private-sector directors I appointed to Coal Corp discovered that the miners had no feedback on how much coal they had mined each day. A board was set up at each mine recording the number of tonnes mined that day. The output increased each day as the miners sought to break their previous record.

When inspecting the Auckland railway yard I noticed a sign very much like those you see by the roadside showing the degree of fire risk – a dashboard-like sign with an arrow. In this case the arrow pointed to damage caused by shunting, ranging from moderate to severe. The arrow was pointing to below moderate; that is, it was so good it was off the chart.

I asked, 'Is this for real?' 'Oh yes,' was the answer. 'How can you have less damage than head office thinks is possible?' 'We could always shunt like this but no one cared before.'

Studies show over and over that just knowing that your job matters and that some one notices how well you are working and says so makes a significant difference.

Most managers manage by exception. They look for what is wrong. The most dramatic example I saw of this was in communist Vietnam. The penalty for a mistake was the salt mines or the Vietnamese equivalent. There was no reward for initiative. So there was no initiative.

> The penalty for a mistake was the salt mines or the Vietnamese equivalent. There was no reward for initiative. So there was no initiative.

It is not enough to have fine-sounding mission statements if the infrastructure is negative. I found at the Auckland kindergarten association that we not only had a wonderful mission statement that said we recognised the partnership with Maori in the Treaty, but that before each meeting we also stood and recited our multicultural mission (I am not kidding); and the association even had a Treaty officer to ensure we were politically correct.

Yet we had to close the Otara kindergarten that had the highest proportion of Maori children. Under the employment agreement with the union we had to advertise each job and then employ the most senior teacher who applied, regardless of whether that applicant was suitable. Teachers could and did apply for multiple positions and the most senior could be appointed to a number of jobs; that teacher would then select the one she wanted and the rest were re-advertised. In two years no one had taken up the Otara position.

We could not afford to keep paying for relieving teachers. Our mission statement was to improve Maori education; our culture was to preserve rules that favoured senior teachers. Teachers got an automatic pay rise for every year they taught no matter how well they did this. A senior teacher could get paid more than a principal who had significant responsibilities. So we had a shortage of teachers willing to be principals and a tradition of teachers declining to work a minute extra.

The award paid fourteen days' sick leave that teachers had to use or lose. A medical miracle: most teachers were sick two weeks a year. However, there were some teachers who caught an illness from the children – hepatitis is an occupational hazard – but after two weeks they received no further support.

In contrast, in a private-sector firm we had unlimited sick leave and almost no absenteeism. I recall that we kept a secretary who had contracted a serious illness on full pay for six months.

One of the things we did in the kindergarten association was to negotiate our own employment agreement so we could pay our principal teachers more and employ staff because they had the skills we needed. The union called a strike against us paying more than the national award!

What we were really doing was changing the culture so that the reality of work matched our lofty mission.

> Too many firms become bureaucracies where form rather than substance matters. Their employees quickly learn that their efforts do not matter.

Mainfreight's culture is the reason for the firm's success.

I am sure that one of the reasons Mainfreight is such a success story is that every one who works for the firm knows it is possible to start at the bottom and reach the top. Indeed, the firm starts its graduates off at the bottom on the theory that if you want to manage, it helps to actually know how to do the jobs you are managing.

I am convinced that it is the poor 'infrastructure' of organisations which leads managers to become authoritarian and staff to become rule followers. Too many firms become bureaucracies where form rather than substance matters. Their employees quickly learn that their efforts do not matter.

The art of negotiation

ONE WAY TO persuade reluctant employees to make improvements is by negotiation. This can be done individually or as an organisation.

Stephen Franks, ACT's justice spokesman until the 2005 election, was a little disturbed by my forceful style, being used to the more conciliatory style of a major law firm. I think he found equally disturbing my reluctance to put issues to the vote but instead to allow some discussions to carry on for months.

It is a modification of Michael Gourley's saying: 'effective decisions equal quality times acceptance'. Some decisions need to be made at once. Others are not urgent and a leader can allow time for the organisation to think it through and reach a consensus. The art is to know which issue is which. To Stephen, the more important the issue, the more urgent the decision. To me, it was often the opposite. If the issue was important it was worth taking time to get it right and time to take the whole caucus with us.

The right of leaders to chair caucus and the prime minister to chair Cabinet is one of the few powers leaders have. Party leaders I have served under would never give it up. David Lange, a brilliant chair, could direct a debate just by the order in which he called the speakers.

I decided to agree with Stephen's request and have the chair of caucus rotate. It seemed to me that the quid pro quo was worth it. Chairing the caucus forced MPs to look at issues the way the leader must. At the very least, it improves caucus attendance. Really important issues require 100 per cent attendance. Stephen, in the chair, found that he could not force the caucus to make decisions before it was ready to do so.

You can negotiate change one to one. For example, I am a walking hurricane. Papers seem to go everywhere to the despair of my staff. My private secretary used to call at my home to go though my suit pockets to find papers. My solution was to agree that my secretary was in charge of all papers in the office and could organise them in any way she chose. I promised never to file a paper or to make any suggestions as to how to organise the paperwork, and to follow instructions to clear urgent paperwork. In return I expected the office to produce any paper I want when I wanted it. It worked well.

> The art of negotiation is a critical management skill in business and politics alike.

The art of negotiation is a critical management skill in business and politics alike. I am not a natural negotiator, as a series of disastrous car purchases prove. Negotiation is a

THE ART OF NEGOTIATION

Yet another formal photograph in China
with the late Malcolm McConnell.

skill you can learn. Some people see negotiation as screwing as much as possible out of the opposition. There is a better way. Malcolm McConnell taught me that a certain generosity of approach produced dividends all round.

McConnell International was offered what appeared to be a wonderful contract to do civil engineering for a major new port in China. It appeared to be a very profitable contract involving years of work.

'I do not understand how the Chinese are ever going to recover the cost,' said Malcolm.

'That'd be their worry, wouldn't it?' I replied breezily. I was young, then.

'In my experience, when clients discover they have made a mistake they always want to renegotiate the contract,' said Malcolm, 'Then it becomes our worry too.' A Singapore engineering firm was the lead contractor and Malcolm got me to go home via Singapore to ask them how they thought the scheme would ever pay.

'It will never make a return,' they told me when we met up. 'It's an economic white elephant.'

'Why are you involved?' I asked.

'We are government-owned and we have been ordered to do work in China,' was the rather glum reply. 'Has your government ordered you to go to China?'

I said that the New Zealand Government didn't tell us where to invest. The Singaporean explained that they had been promised extra investment from the national superannuation scheme to cover any losses. They thought it would be many millions of dollars. (I have had my doubts about compulsory government superannuation schemes ever since. You just can't trust politicians with your money; they can't resist using it for politics.) 'If you don't have to be involved, why are you?' the Singaporean asked me. It was a good question. No one would have asked it if Malcolm McConnell hadn't looked at the deal from the other side. We saved a lot of aggravation by declining the contract.

I was the negotiator for the Lange Government. Not because I was a good negotiator, but because I never learnt how to avoid the job. When the government needed to negotiate Maori claims, aviation agreements, new forestry contracts or industrial disputes, the job was delegated to me. As a result, I had a whole conga line of angry New Zealanders filing into my office: young doctors, airline pilots, nurses, seamen, meat workers . . .

From the experience, I formulated some rules of successful negotiation.

The best outcomes occur when both parties look upon the negotiation as a problem-solving exercise. You agree on the objectives, you discuss alternatives and see what fits from both points of view. Negotiation becomes collaborative.

You can get through anything if the parties want to settle. If they don't, human beings will argue about anything; the venue, the sitting, and the procedure.

It was always my first question at the first meeting: 'Do you want to settle or don't you?' If the answer was in any way equivocal, I would say, 'Come back when you want a deal.' Usually this produced a quick change of stance, but not always. It is a waste of time negotiating if the parties do not want to agree as any one who has done marriage counselling can verify.

When the parties did indicate that they wanted to settle, I would ask if they were mandated to do a settlement. It's all too common that people say they have to report back to their boss, board, federation or members.

> The best outcomes occur when both parties look upon the negotiation as a problem-solving exercise. You agree on the objectives, you discuss alternatives and see what fits from both points of view. Negotiation becomes collaborative.

I would say, 'Go away and get a mandate or send someone who can agree.' Very often, the lack of a mandate means the other party is just on a sniff-and-learn exercise. The effect of forcing the mandate issue, forces the party to decide if they want a deal.

I can't emphasise it enough: if the parties don't want to reach an agreement you are wasting your time.

> If the parties don't want to reach an agreement you are wasting your time.

Another excuse not to negotiate is the claim that whoever opens negotiations always has the weaker hand. This assumes that all negotiations result in one winner and a loser. Constructive achievers are proactive. They take the initiative, they create the momentum, and things go their way. They are always trying to figure out how to improve things. Always suggesting win–win deals.

Port reform in New Zealand may have been highly desirable but no one had managed it in fifty years. We had a situation where unskilled wharfies, working an average thirteen hours a week, were earning as much as doctors. Or more accurately, as much as brain surgeons. The wharfies weren't interested in a deal from the employers because the only deal on offer was: work harder and faster for less money.

The industry just would not face up to the size of the redundancy package needed to get a deal. But that was purely a perception problem. The figures actually all pointed the other way. They showed that, huge as the payments were, the payback was in many cases in less than twelve months, a more than 100 per cent return. The industry was happy to invest in port cranes that had a 10 per cent rate of return but baulked at a payment that would pay for itself in a year.

While we copped criticism from Federated Farmers and some employer groups, the decision to 'buy the jobs' changed the environment. Port reform could then be negotiated without strikes.

The ports were one thing but shipping crews were another.

When I had been retired by the voters, newly privatised railways asked for my advice on how to achieve sensible manning levels on the rail ferries, a hotbed of industrial strife. The crew's conditions were unbelievable. One perk they enjoyed was to be able to live anywhere in New Zealand and be flown to Wellington to go to work. They were so highly paid and worked for so little time that some crew lived overseas.

The rail ferries are a vital transport link. The South Island is economically dependent on the service. The reality is that the country cannot afford a stoppage of any length of time; the economic damage is too great. No wonder the seamen had the power to negotiate terms like that.

I gave the board my assessment: 'Unless you are willing to replace the total crew of each ferry with a "scab" crew there is no way the unions will ever negotiate a sensible contact. Everyone in the maritime industry knows the present agreement is an outrage. In Australia you can recruit replacement crews. The ferries' conditions are so good, I guarantee we can recruit seamen willing to work in a lockout.'

The board accepted my recommendation provided I would lead the negotiations. I have to say I would have done it for nothing. I regarded it as unfinished business. I had never had a chance to tackle the ferries, as the unions never went on strike while I was minister. As Dave Morgan, the secretary of the seaman's union, put it, 'We were never going to give you an excuse.'

We negotiated a new internationally competitive agreement that saved rail twenty-one million a year, without a strike, and this is how it happened.

The union secretaries had nicknames like Marmite (a little bit goes a long way), and Twiggy (a grossly fat steward). I rang him to say, 'Twiggy, as a courtesy I am just letting you know that I am negotiating the new rail ferry contract.' He claimed that he lost a stone that week (no one noticed).

These ferry negotiations present the toughest situation; one party has everything and is determined not to negotiate. Why would it? We were helped by one thing – a new fast ferry service had gone into competition. I gave the facts and figures that showed how the competition was hurting us and that our situation was not sustainable. Jobs were ultimately at risk.

I knew from experience that the unions would argue safety and claim the proposed crewing levels were not realistic. So off we went to see for ourselves. The negotiating team went to visit Europe and inspect the English Channel ferries. Our names must be on some Interpol alert as we crossed the Channel on four different ferries in two days, driving like lunatics from port to port. We looked at how each ferry handled docking, loading cars, serving passengers and how they covered emergency evacuations.

We took the best of what we saw in each operation and realised the manning could be reduced by over half. As the European ferries have to meet stringent EC safety terms it was very powerful to say in negotiations, 'We saw what we are proposing on the P&O ferry docking at Dover. We spoke to the officers and men who say it's a safe system. They have never had an accident.'

What we did not say was that we also saw some shocking cases of poor manning and the ancestral European class system in action. On the night ferry that sails from the Netherlands to England, each crew job was given to a different nationality strictly according to the national stereotype. The officers were efficient Germans. The cooks were French. The engineers were Scots. The waiters Philippine, and the laundry was run by Chinese. The masters of arms were British ex-Marine military police.

I asked the captain, who spoke perfect English, for an explanation and he did not see anything funny about this racial stereotyping. But then he had a Teutonic sense of humour.

'We have to have the British ex-military police because they are so tough,' he said with a mixture of awe and horror. 'Only they can handle the English football hooligans.' He showed me how the ex-military police would frogmarch the hooligans to the brig, an iron cage. Then they turn the sea hoses on them: freezing water from the North Sea. Even the hooligans can't take much of that. 'When we land, the marines take the soccer hooligans to the top of the gang plank and throw them down. We never prosecute and they never complain. We could not treat any other European national that way,' he said shaking his head in wonder. 'We must have the English on board to handle the English. They are barbarians.'

We had our own national stereotypes of the English trade unionist. Most of the unionists I was negotiating with were English. They implicitly believed that the English were best and accepted that if P&O ferries were doing something it must be right. (They sometimes mused about what must have happened to their comrades to agree to such an arrangement.)

If we had not met the union's legitimate concerns about safety, there would have been no deal.

In the course of the negotiations, which involved me taking a number of ferry trips to see for myself, I realised our ferries were unsafe. The seamen's union had weekly meetings of all shop stewards. An informal arrangement had arisen whereby the union delegates didn't do anything as reckless as put to sea, and as a result every ferry sailed short-crewed. The officers didn't do a crew count. The captain explained that if he did, the crew would strike. I tried to do my own informal count and realised that our ferry was short by a number of crew. As there was, formally, twice the crew that were needed, this shortage probably improved efficiency. On the other hand, in a sinking ship you don't want to be looking for crew who were on the crew list but not on board.

We made it clear that they would have to follow the

safety regulations and there would be crew counts in future. The weekly union meeting would have to go. Only a government organisation can ignore the law because they know no government will allow itself to be prosecuted. Because governments write the law, bureaucrats know they can always rewrite the law. If necessary, retrospectively!

The superb negotiating team that New Zealand Rail had put together made our task possible. We told the unions that we had to make the changes and if need be, we would lock them out and run the ferries with a scab crew. The unions didn't believe us so we had our recruits brought across in secret and located in a motel in Masterton about eighty kilometres from Wellington. I had expected the crew to be immediately spotted. It was only when we brought them out to do their life-raft drills in Wellington harbour that the union negotiators accepted the replacement crew was real. They still did not think we would do it.

Adults only learn from experience so we served lockout notices.

Adults only learn from experience so we served lockout notices. The unions filed a notice to challenge the lockout's legality. The industrial court sat in an emergency hearing in front of Judge Goddard. Lockouts are very rare. The legislation had been never tested in court. I was sure that I could rely on Judge Goddard to find some reason for deciding our notice was invalid, but we had to impress on the union we were for real.

OUT OF THE RED

(*Laurence Clark, Alexander Turnbull Library, Wellington, NZ, H-102-013*)

The judge ran true to form and ruled that service of the notice could not be done by registered mail. We had to serve each crew member personally. A summons to court where you can lose your liberty can be affected by registered mail but a notice by your employer of a lockout, that's on TV news and the front page of every newspaper, has to be delivered in person, according to the industrial court. In a later case the Court of Appeal reversed this silly ruling.

At any rate, the case got me what I wanted: time to negotiate and the unions possessed of the knowledge that they had to negotiate.

But personal service presented us with a real problem. Process-servers had to identify and serve each and every crew member. There are a significant number of ferrymen who'd like to string old judge Goddard up by his own intestines for his thoughtfulness. The old saying of a wife in every port turned out to be true, and quite a number of divorces came out of the process-serving.

A process-server would arrive at a home to be told, 'He is at work.'

The reply would be 'We are from work; we know he is here, we will just wait so he may as well accept service.' The reluctant crew member would eventually appear from the pub, or the track, or his other home and other wife.

We were also faced with the problem that in order to meet the judge's instructions it would be necessary to serve the crews on duty. Going on board to serve a lockout notice to a militant crew member at the bottom of a ship who did not want to be served was a risky endeavour.

I offered to stand on the wharf and shout 'I am here, come and get me!' As the crew rushed down the gangplank we could hit them with the documents and say, 'You are served'. The consensus was it would work but I would not survive. There are still those who think we should have taken the risk.

The negotiating team decided that they would deliver the notices themselves. I have to admit I was relieved when they refused my offer to go with them. They said my presence would be too provocative. I think the seaman appreciated the courage of our team. It went without a hitch.

Nonetheless, there were punches thrown, and there were bruises.

There is a bit of an art to getting through a picket line, so let me tell you what it is, just in case you have to do it yourself.

> There is a bit of an art to getting through a picket line, so let me tell you what it is, just in case you have to do it yourself.

You walk along the line looking for someone you know holding a placard. 'Hi Bob,' you say, putting out your arm. Normal human reactions usually take over. Bob will take his hand off the pole holding the sign that reads, 'Prebble out' and before he realises it, he is shaking my hand as I grip him tightly and walk towards him, turning him sideways creating a gap in the picket line. I walk though. I am in and out before anyone reacts. Unfortunately when this did happen, those following me hesitated and were spat at and punched.

> You never do know what the other party needs and you are often surprised. Often you can accommodate the request.

It is my view that in negotiations you should not just make demands. You actively seek to see if there are things that the other side wants that you can accommodate. You never do know what the other party needs and you are often surprised. Often you can accommodate the request.

'Rail wants to be a good employer. Is there anything, outside our bottom-line requests, we can do?' To a group who had everything this was a difficult request. Finally the seamen said that they would like a bigger allowance of laundry powder. I promised to investigate. I rang the man in charge of stores. 'Can we give the crew more washing powder?' 'What do they do with it?' was the reply. 'We are issuing kilos of laundry powder now and we have a free laundry service on board. We buy so much we get it in twenty-kilo sacks,' he exclaimed. I went home and calculated that my large family used less than a quarter of the washing powder being issued per crew member. I reported back that this was another rort that would have to end. We settled the negotiations just minutes before the second lockout notice took effect.

It has been my experience in negotiations that each side thinks it knows what the other side wants, but rarely does. Whenever I was called into a negotiation, I would ask each side, 'What do you need? I am not asking what you want. I want to win Lotto, but what I need is enough to pay the mortgage.'

This is crucial in negotiations, to get the parties to distinguish between needs and wants. You should ask yourself first to make sure that you have distinguished between what you must have and what would be nice to have. Then you need to get the other side to tell you their side of it. I would then ask the party, 'What does the other side need and what does it want?' I would

> This is crucial in negotiations, to get the parties to distinguish between needs and wants.

then repeat the exercise with the other party.

Not once did each party know what the other side really needed. Not once. It was not just in employment disputes that both the employers and the unions failed to realise what was crucial to the other side. If I can say what every mother in the country knows: men are so selfish – they only think of themselves.

In commercial negotiations such as those between airlines and airports, forest owners and mills, telephone users and Telecom, both sides were sure they knew what the other side wanted. They were sure they could not meet the other side's needs.

It often came as a revelation to the parties when I told them what the other side really wanted. Often they were happy to meet the request. There was one example of this so egregious that it really needs to be recorded.

I woke up one morning in 1986 to discover that whatever I had been eating didn't agree with me. We won't go into the details, though they are still fresh in my mind. I staggered in to attend a Cabinet committee meeting. Afterwards, the minister of labour started to brief me about the long-running strike at the meat works. The workers were on strike and had then been locked out over a demand by the employers that they be able to use the same floor for sheep and cattle. As I wasn't well I started to fidget, and asked a little impatiently, 'Why are you telling me this?'

He replied 'My plane leaves for Geneva at midday at which point you are acting minister of labour.'

I staggered back to my office now feeling really ill. 'Cancel all my appointments; I am going home to bed.'

THE ART OF NEGOTIATION

At one minute past midday the phone rang and it was my private secretary apologetically saying that the head of the Federation of Labour, Ken Douglas, had telephoned insisting that he meet with me urgently. Could he give him my home telephone number? I croaked that he could and within moments Ken was on the phone. He was in Wellington airport and he had seen Stan's plane leaving. He told me he had lobbied the prime minister to make me acting minister of labour. 'We are desperate to settle this dispute. If we do not act we're going to lose the whole season. We need you to bring the parties together.'

Ken Douglas rang me to help resolve the freezing works 'lockout'.

I replied, thanks to Stan's briefing, that the employers would not settle unless they could use the same equipment for both beef and mutton.

The answer was surprising: 'We know that and we have always been willing to agree.' I asked him to come and see me immediately.

When he arrived, Ken repeated his claim. He said the workers knew the farmers were in real trouble. The government had removed all subsidies. Agriculture was going through a very painful restructuring. He told me the workers feared for their jobs and that they well knew restrictive practices, like having different floors for cattle and sheep, had to go. Ken also said that the workers weren't even seeking a pay rise.

I called the employers' advocate who expressed incredulity and made it clear that the union's assurances were simply not to be believed.

I called Ken back and asked how soon he could get a representative of each union shed in the country into my office. He undertook to do it by the following night. So many men turned up that we met in the Cabinet committee room. I personally put to the union delegates the employers' demands. A number of the delegates were household names for their militancy. Each in turn told me the same thing. 'Richard, we know the industry is in crisis. We realise things have to change. The men had agreed to all the employers' demands even before the lockout.'

I again reported these conversations only to find the employer advocates didn't want to know. Being a minister I was able to ring the chief executives of the biggest meat works and get them to come and see me in parliament. They were almost as obstinate. It was an unintelligible dispute. It was psychotic, in its way. The employers were saying they would continue with the strike until the union agreed to all of their demands – but the demands had already been met. And the season was on the point of being lost.

I finally broke the strike by telling the employers that as a minister I would have to go on television and tell the farmers that the strike, which was costing them millions, was totally unnecessary.

THE ART OF NEGOTIATION

For years the meat works had given in to outrageous union demands. The farmers, facing a much tougher environment, had served notice on the meat works to get tough. The meat works managers needed the strike to show how tough they were.

Make sense to you? To me neither. It happened all the time.

Boards

I HAVE CHAIRED boards, served on boards, and appointed directors to twenty-odd companies with a combined capitalisation greater than the stock market. I've been in, around or on boards all my adult life – Cabinet, statutory, state-owned enterprise, public company, private company, trust, education, sport and community. Boards are the single most significant collective in our society. Boards are how things happen. Good boards may not guarantee success, but no organisation will prosper long if the board is bad.

I would never appoint a green, 26-year-old lawyer to my first board – but then I was elected, not appointed. It was to the board of the Portage licensing trust in the early 1970s. The trust was a contradiction in terms: the only way we could make money was by selling liquor and that was the one thing we had been elected to prevent. Certainly, we opposed every restaurant we could that wanted the right to sell wine with a meal – but on the other hand we tried to start a Coronation Street-style local pub culture. We also got into the business of running radio stations. Despite having a monopoly on the sale of alcohol – normally considered a licence to print money – the board almost went bankrupt. The lack of clarity was very instructive – I apologise for making you pay for the tuition.

While most boards know what their statutory duties are, I believe that improving board performance would lift New Zealand's economy.

Personally, I don't believe that the fashionable theory that independent directors guarantee good governance is correct. Two of the best boards I have served on had the chief executive as the chairman. You can't do that today. In some of the poorest boards I have served on, all the directors were independent. It didn't help. The rules don't help. There's only one rule to which I've found no exceptions at all: if you ask a question of someone and they reply by saying: 'How long is a piece of string?' you should never, ever give that that person any responsibility.

When I was retired by the voters I told a newspaper reporter that one of the things I had missed in life was never serving on a school board. The board of the Auckland Kindergarten Association got to hear about this unguarded comment at a sensitive moment. It was meeting the following Thursday and had been told that its ninety-nine kindergartens were in deficit to the tune of half a million dollars, and that they were

Valedictory speech, July 2005. (*Dominion Post*)

all individually liable for the sum. They decided to co-opt me. We were the happy few headed into the breach. Within the year, half a dozen middle-class housewives, a small businessman and I had the association in the black. How? Incentives? Not really. Assembling all the facts? A bit, but not fundamentally. Achievement thinking? Sort of. Our great success from which all else flowed was that we appointed a good chief executive.

Appointing a good chief executive is 90 per cent of any board's task.

It is the first and fundamental skill you look for in a director. None of the women on the kindergarten board had any of the skills that it is fashionable to look for in a director. Yet they recognised a good executive when they found her.

No amount of skill with figures, no experience in business, no ability to make money, can overcome an inability on the part of a board to appoint a good chief executive or to recognise when to get a new one.

Most boards that fail do so because they have the wrong leader. You've got to be able to move leaders on when it's time. It doesn't matter very often but when it does, it matters a lot. Oddly enough, I never did much in the way of firing chairmen. I found by chatting to them that they were well aware of the gap between the demand on their abilities and the supply. Provided they were

> **Appointing a good chief executive is 90 per cent of any board's task.**

allowed a dignified exit (the arts always needed directors) they were often willing to leave Giant Co. and support the opera. The larger problem was their wives; that's why New Zealand needs an honours system – to noisily reward people while quietly relieving them of their duties.

It's more difficult getting to grips with the problem of the manager who is not quite making it, who possibly could make it, and is asking for another year to have a go at making it. I can think of very few examples of regret at not giving the extra year. I also have a number of examples of regret at allowing it. But I've got a number of examples when the extra year turned out apples for everyone.

Michael Morris, for instance, had turned in some dreadful figures for New Zealand Post and I suggested to him he might want to move on to some grazing. He said, not unreasonably, that these figures were delivering exactly what Jonathan Hunt had asked for. If I wanted an efficient postal service he could deliver that too – and that's exactly what he did.

Obviously, you need the obvious things in directors. You need people who can fulfil the duties set out in the Companies Act.

It's also good to have at least one person for whom figures sing; a person who understands the law; a person who knows that particular business, and people who have successfully run businesses before. It all helps, but above all you need people who can do more than this, who can make sure that achievement thinking is allowed to flourish, that achievable goals can be set and met, and that the culture exists to support both these requirements.

BOARDS

Even after all my expensive board experience, I do not claim to be a natural director. I have just learnt some good questions to ask. As I say, there are no fixed and permanent rules of where to look and how you get what you want. Good people can produce poor results. Talented people can fail. People with strength, courage and diligence can go the wrong way.

What do we need? What is it that makes the difference? Most of all I looked for judgement.

But how do you assess that? Professional directors are going to make an excellent first impression. That's what they're good at. They always have very impressive CVs. But then, my 21-year-old has an impressive CV. Assessing people is very difficult.

My friend Mike had judgement. He left his law job and joined a large corporate, starting off in their personnel department. He had no professional or academic qualifications for the post nor had he any idea what to do or not to do, or when to do it or not. Within two years he was running the division. He had six months of grace. He had time to watch the members of the group discussing strategy. He noticed that one or two of the group members were invariably right, one or two were invariably wrong and that most people wavered in the in-between. Mike merely remembered what was said. He noted who turned out to be right and who turned out to be wrong. The people who were usually right were usually right about everything. So he agreed with the people who were usually right, and when necessary acted on their advice. At his most successful, he was still claiming he had no idea how the business worked. What he taught

> There is no point in asking for advice unless you intend to take it. Most people who ask for advice are actually asking for reassurance.

me became one of my maxims: there is no point in asking for advice unless you intend to take it. Most people who ask for advice are actually asking for reassurance. Mike worked out who gave good advice – and then he sought it out and took it. People loved him for it.

But when you don't have six months? How can you tell whether people are any good at what they're doing?

There's one way of identifying people who aren't, for whatever reason, pulling their weight. Very often it isn't their fault but that of their boss. When you know who isn't producing you have at least the option of giving them something useful to do.

New Zealand Rail needed some help reorganising its workshops. It brought over the former chief engineer of Conrail from America. This elderly gentleman rolled through the depot chatting to people as he went. At the end of the day he summoned the managers and told them how many staff they could lose, and what their names were. Our guys were astonished because every name he gave them rang true. How did he do it? 'I just asked people what their job consisted of. Those that could tell me were obviously doing something useful, those that couldn't, obviously weren't.'

I've found that little question to be invaluable. I ask people – from caretakers to chairmen – to describe their duties. If they can't answer succinctly it's a dime to a dozen they don't know what their job is and that someone else is actually doing the work.

I am looking to see if our 'infrastructure' is supporting a constructive culture. Watching the culture is every bit as important as watching the cash.

The way people talk about their work is very revealing. I ask the achievement-oriented question: 'What is it you do that makes a difference?' A caretaker, for instance, might say his job is one of the most important in the company. The way he keeps the place determines visitors' first impressions of the firm. Then again, another caretaker might say: 'There's no point in keeping this lobby tidy; I pick up the litter and the bums here just mess it up again!'

> 'I just asked people what their job consisted of. Those that could tell me were obviously doing something useful, those that couldn't, obviously weren't.'

Other rules of thumb include these:

- Do the directors know what they're in business for? Is it to be busy – or is it to make a profit? Remember,

Russell McVeigh used to be country's biggest law firm. It no longer has the largest number of partners but has the highest income per partner. Which Russell McVeigh would you rather work for?

- How flat is the organisation's structure? Generally, the flatter the better, so that information flows easily. How accurately has the board identified the performance indicators?

- When things are going wrong who takes the blame? In my experience, public-sector managers were always blaming their computer systems for the larger failure of their enterprise. All they needed was money for a world-leading system. By contrast, the head of technology on a private-sector board I am on said about a new acquisition: 'I have put the computer plans on hold because the information they want to put in it is rubbish. Until I have worked out what the key performance indicators for this company are and we are collecting it accurately, there is absolutely no point in buying a new computer.'

Conclusion

SO, HERE WE are together at the end. We've come quite a way. I hope you've enjoyed the reading as much as I have the writing. I think we have discovered why some succeed and others fail. It's not that surprising. At the bottom of it all is culture. You create the company culture and then the culture creates the company. And we've seen how successful organisations encourage cause-and-effect thinking and generate an achievement culture.

It is New Zealand's contribution to the world. We took 10 per cent of the economy that was an economic basket case, with thousands of employees with a negative, angry culture and transformed the culture and so changed the companies into world-class enterprises.

> At the bottom of it all is culture. You create the company culture and then the culture creates the company.

No other explanation fits the facts. If the SOE model was the whole explanation, TVNZ wouldn't have lost a billion dollars in value over the last six years.

New Zealand has shown we can take the ideas of modern business and apply them to government – indeed to any organisation, even a political party – with spectacular results. ACT had less than 1 per cent of the vote when I became leader. I applied the techniques of Human Synergistics and ACT's vote lifted in every election. And what about the last election? That's another story, for another book.

Let me leave you with this question. What would happen if we were to apply the techniques of an achievement culture in our schools, our health system, our social welfare system and all aspects of life?

What would happen to your company? Your party? Your school? Your hospital? Is it one of the estimated 15 per cent of organisations that have a successful culture? The odds are against it.

To find out, take the culture test in the appendix.

Remember that you can change the way you look at and react to the world. You can choose whether to believe in luck and fate or you can determine to create your own future.

Good luck!

Test your organisation

HOW DOES YOUR company, organisation, government department, sports club, political party, or any organisation you like, measure up in the culture stakes?

The following, I hasten to advise, is not one of Human Synergistics' surveys. I have taken the questions from the writings of Cooke and Lafferty. This is a fun survey to give you more of an understanding of the ideas in this book. To get a valid reading of your organisation's culture you would need to use one of Human Synergistics market-tested surveys.

Note: Even though this is not a Human Synergistics survey, the material describing the culture styles is copyright and is owned by Human Synergistics International.*

Thinking about your organisation
Circle a number to select your response, ranging from 1 = not at all to 6 = to a very great extent

---

* Researched and developed by Robert A Cooke and J Clayton Lafferty. © Copyright Human Synergistics International Ltd.

OUT OF THE RED

To what extent are people expected or implicitly required to exhibit the following behaviours:

1. To be supportive, constructive, and open to influence in their dealings with one another?

   1   2   3   4   5   6

2. To be friendly, open, and sensitive to the satisfaction of their work group?

   1   2   3   4   5   6

3. To feel that they should agree with, gain the approval of, and be liked by others?

   1   2   3   4   5   6

4. To conform, follow the rules, and make a good impression?

   1   2   3   4   5   6

5. To do only what they are told and to clear all decisions with superiors?

   1   2   3   4   5   6

6. To shift responsibility to others and avoid any possibility of being blamed for a mistake?

   1   2   3   4   5   6

7. To gain status and influence by being critical and to oppose the ideas of others?

   1   2   3   4   5   6

TEST YOUR ORGANISATION

8 To feel they will be rewarded for taking charge, controlling subordinates and, at the same time, being responsive to the demands of superiors?

    1   2   3   4   5   6

9 To operate in a 'win–lose' framework and believe they must work against (rather than with) their peers to be noticed?

    1   2   3   4   5   6

10 To feel they must avoid any mistakes, keep track of everything, and work long hours to attain narrowly defined objectives?

    1   2   3   4   5   6

11 To set challenging but realistic goals, establish plans to reach these goals, and pursue them with enthusiasm?

    1   2   3   4   5   6

12 To gain enjoyment from their work, develop themselves, and take on new and interesting activities?

    1   2   3   4   5   6

The results of your survey follow.

Your results

THE DIAGRAM ON the next page sets out the culture of the organisation.

To enter the results, mark your answers 1 to 6, 1 being the bull's eye and 6 the outer ring. You can then connect the lines, shading in the diagram from the centre.

The style numbers correspond with the sections of the circumplex. For example, if you answered 6 for the first question (style one), then colour in section 1 (top right hand side) from the sixth line (i.e. the outside line of the circle) to the middle. And so on around the circumplex.

If your organisation scores highly on the constructive styles (styles 1, 2, 11 and 12), then you see the organisation's culture as primarily constructive. It is an environment that stimulates people's needs for growth and achievement. There is a balance between concern for people and concern for tasks. The organisation encourages the attainment of both personal and organisational goals though a co-operative effort.

Humanistic-encouraging. Characterises organisations that are managed in a participative and person-centred way.

YOUR RESULTS

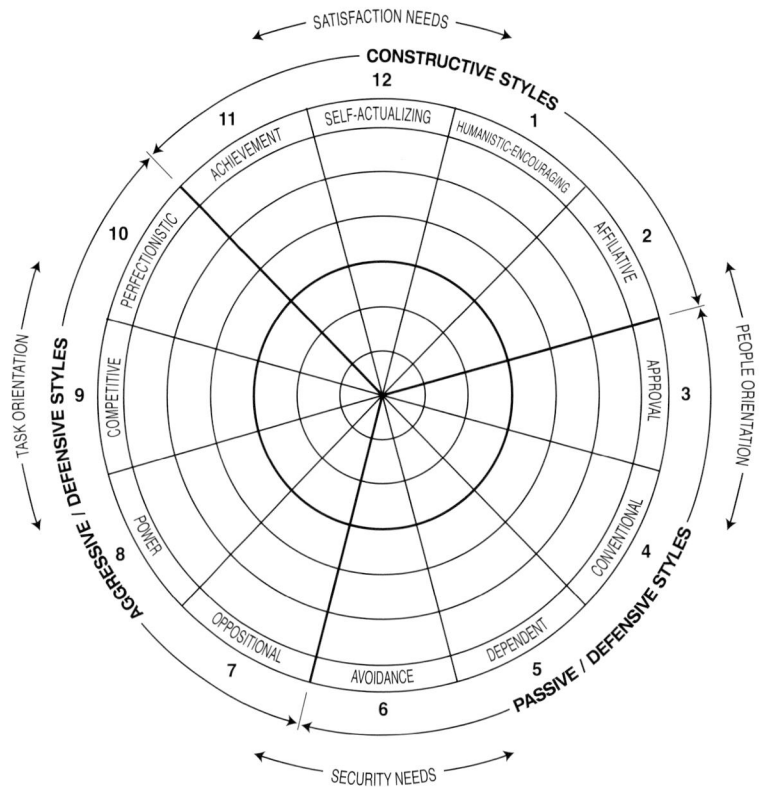

The Organisational Culture Inventory Circumplex
Source: Reprinted by permission. Copyright © 1987–2005 held by Human Synergistics International.
Research and development by Robert A. Cooke (Ph.D.) and J. Clayton Lafferty, (Ph.D)

Affiliative. Members are expected to place a high priority on constructive interpersonal relationships.

Achievement. People are expected to pursue a standard of excellence and work for the sense of accomplishment

Self-actualising. Characterises organisations that value creativity, quality over quantity, and both task accomplishment and individual growth.

Congratulations. Less than one company in five has this culture. Dr Robert Cooke's research indicates that these styles represent the most successful cultures.

If you scored your organisation high in the passive/defensive cluster (styles 3–6), you see the organisation as having policies that lead staff to feel insecure or apprehensive, controlled and restrained. People are uneasy about their relationships with other employees. The feeling is that it is better to 'play it safe'.

Approval. This describes organisations in which conflicts are avoided and interpersonal relationships are pleasant – at least superficially.

Conventional. This style is descriptive of organisations that are conservative, traditional, and bureaucratically controlled.

Dependent. This style is descriptive of organisations that are hierarchically controlled and non-participative.

Avoidance. This style characterises organisations that fail to reward success but nevertheless punish mistakes.

Your organisation has real problems. These styles create very unsuccessful cultures and yet are the most common in central and local government; unfortunately also very common in education.

If you scored your organisation high in the aggressive/defensive cluster (styles 7–10), you see the organisation following strategies that lead employees to feel anxious about their status, worry about how they are performing compared with others and fixated on short-term performance. The organisation is more concerned about tasks than people, which leads people to put their own needs ahead of those of the organisation or other team members. It is every man and woman for themself.

Dr Robert Cook, whose research proves it's culture that counts.

Oppositional. This style describes organisations in which confrontation prevails and negativism is rewarded.

Power. This style is descriptive of non-participative organisations structured on the basis of the authority inherent in member's positions.

Competitive. This culture is one in which winning is valued and members are rewarded for out-performing one another.

Perfectionistic. This style of culture characterises organisations in which perfectionism, persistence and hard work are valued.

These styles represent the most common types of culture in business. For a short time, aggressive firms can achieve spectacular results but often fail because they cannot adapt to change.

If you are a manager of an organisation that has a negative culture, Human Synergistics research shows it is possible to change the culture.

Their advice is very practical. Look at the culture profile and target an area where your efforts could make a difference. Start by encouraging people's development. You can start with just one person's development.

Caution

If you are a manager and you have just done this survey and you are feeling pretty pleased with the results, it is probably because, like me, you have done a rosy self-analysis of your organisation.

Human Synergistics has surveyed thousands of senior executives and found managers intend to be constructive, think that they are, and believe that they are heading a constructive organisation.

When employees are surveyed it often reveals a very different culture.

But here is a real test. Use the Human Synergistics organisational culture inventory.

When peers, those who report to them and those they report to, are surveyed, it reveals a disconnect between

YOUR RESULTS

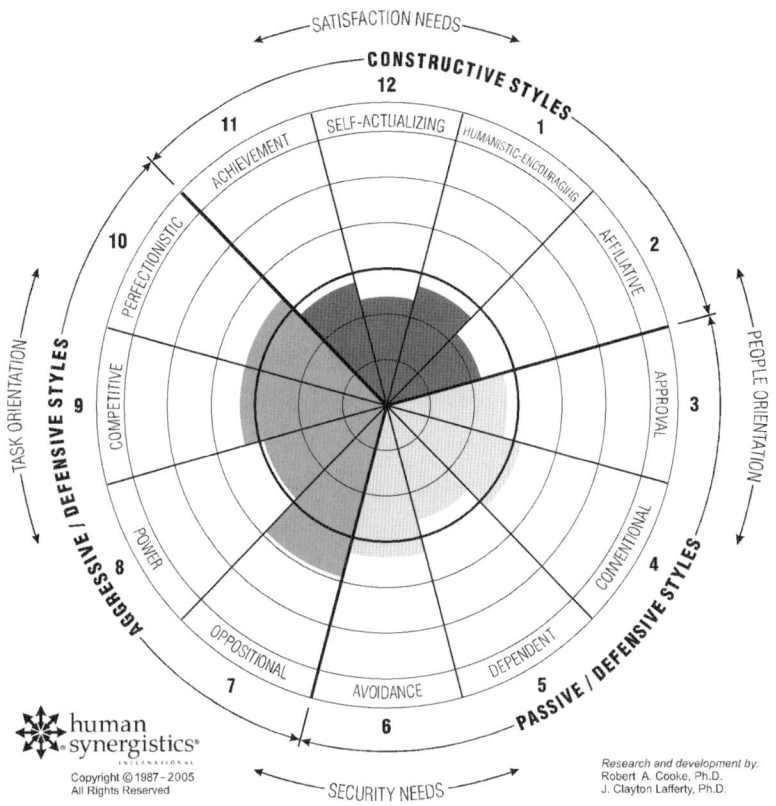

A description of the organisational culture of
New Zealand companies as described by 43,000 members
– we have some work to do to improve performance.

what managers intended as an organisational culture and the actual culture.

Most organisations are typically aggressive/defensive and many are passive/defensive.

The research shows that it is what others perceive to be your leadership style that is important in influencing the culture.

Do you want to know the truth?

Give the Human Synergistics leadership/impact survey to your boss, those who are your peers and those who report directly to you. Ask them to do the survey, but this time they are not assessing the organisation but your leadership style.

The questionnaire this time asks, 'To what extent do I expect each of the following behaviours from those who work with me?' If the survey comes back showing you have a constructive impact, then you belong to a group that includes just 15 per cent of leaders.

If it comes back showing your leadership produces an aggressive or defensive impact on others, you are joining the 85 per cent rest of us and, like us, you have some work to do.

There is another test. Do people smile when you approach or do they look apprehensive? Mike Bassett claimed he had seen messengers in parliament, who, when they saw me coming, hid in doorways. Hearing this, I was so shocked I consciously changed my style and to my pleasure the messengers at least looked as if they were pleased to see me. Did it matter? Well the messengers made sure I always had a glass of water and when you are speaking that can be rather vital.

When I gave my valedictory speech to parliament I noticed

YOUR RESULTS

to my surprise that all the galleries were full. The whole house, including the press gallery and the messengers gave me a standing ovation. Something I have had only seen twice in my twenty-seven years in parliament. Maybe I have learnt to apply some of the lessons in this book but then they may have been so pleased to see me go.

It is time for us to go.

If it can work for me, it should work for you.

(*Courtesy of Daryl Crimp*)

These books can be ordered from Richard Prebble's website, **www.richardprebble.com**

I've been thinking describes the tumultuous years when Richard Prebble helped reform New Zealand's bankrupt economy. The stories of waste and bureaucratic entanglements and the transformation of the economy to wealth generation are extraordinary.

I've been writing describes the state of New Zealand in 1999 and draws a number of interesting conclusions on what is happening and what is needed for a prosperous future. The egregious behaviours of the 'Treaty industry', how welfare has trashed the values of New Zealanders in one generation and how the rights of criminals have been placed ahead of law-abiding citizens are all described and commented on in detail.

What Happens Next describes the turbulent new parliament in the first term of MMP in 1997. This was the year of the extraordinary coalition that started off with high hopes. With the canny insight only an experienced insider can give, Richard Prebble will surprise you with his insight into the behaviour of our representatives.

Now it's time to act is an update of Richard Prebble's best seller *I've been thinking*, with new material and a round-up of the events since that first book.

Closing the Gaps. Thoughtful and insightful writings by the members of the ACT Caucus, 2001. Includes: *New Zealand – Tenth by 2010*, Richard Prebble (CBE); *Health and ACC*, Hon Ken Shirley; *Justice for All*, Stephen Franks; *Free Trade: Route to Poverty or Growth*, Rodney Hide MP (Leader of the ACT Party); *Welfare Reform: For the Sake of our Children*, Muriel Newman; *Tomorrows Agriculture*, Penny Webster; *Local Government*, Owen Jennings.

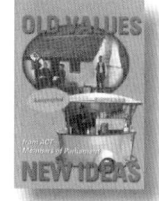

Old Values New Ideas. More thoughtful and insightful writings by the members of the ACT Caucus, 2002. Includes: *Old Values, New Ideas*, Richard Prebble (CBE); *The Kyoto Protocol*, Hon Ken Shirley; *How should ACT treat the Treaty*, Stephen Franks; *Free Trade: Route to Poverty or Growth*, Rodney Hide, MP (Leader of the ACT Party); *For the General Welfare*, Muriel Newman; *City of Snails*, Penny Webster.

Liberal Thinking. Even more thoughtful and insightful writings by the members of the ACT Caucus, 2003. Includes: *Why I Do Not Vote National*, Richard Prebble (CBE); *New Zealand's No-Nuke Nonsense*, Hon Ken Shirley; *Liberals and the Law*, Stephen Franks; *The Classical Liberal View*, Rodney Hide MP (Leader of the ACT Party); *ACT's Welfare Vision*, Muriel Newman; *Property and the Environment*, Gerry Eckhoff; *Crime and Punishment*, Deborah Coddington; *Health for All*, Heather Roy.